Practical Thoughts on Human Resources Management

S. Cihangir Kavuncu

authorHOUSE®

AuthorHouse™ UK
1663 Liberty Drive
Bloomington, IN 47403 USA
www.authorhouse.co.uk
Phone: 0800.197.4150

Published by AuthorHouse 05/10/2018

ISBN: 978-1-5462-8604-2 (sc)
ISBN: 978-1-5462-8605-9 (hc)
ISBN: 978-1-5462-8603-5 (e)

Contents

To my beloved wife and son.

All I know is that I know nothing.
—Socrates

Preface

For a certain time, I was trying to be helpful with my tips for human resources employees by tweeting about human resources. I also started providing explanations after realizing that some of my tweets were not very well understood or that the comments went in a different direction than what I intended, but space was limited, and it was a difficult process of writing. My dear friend Erhan Erkut encouraged me by saying, "Why don't you publish your tweets in a book?" With that confidence, I took the initiative in this matter, and I collected them into a book in such a way that it combines my experience in the human resources field with practices that I used in the past.

I desired to convey everything I know to human resources employees by collecting all the tweets, compiling them in a way that is easy and understandable. This is not a theory book or a book in which I completely transfer my experiences. It is a combination of both of these methods. I hope it will be a useful book that provides you with guidance.

The original book, published in Turkish under the title *5N1İK*, was released almost two years ago. I decided to translate and take the opportunity to add some material and eliminate other material that not fit the international reality. So I would say this book is an extended version of the original Turkish one.

I sincerely thank dear Erhan, who gave me the idea and the courage to write this book, and to my brother and sister from YGA, Özlem Güney and Sadık Ünlü, who worked with me and contributed more than I did on each page for the Turkish version of this book. Without them, this book would have never existed. Also, I also give my endless appreciation to Müge Arslan and Aslı Özçelik, who did my book's pre-reading, and to Orhan Velidedeoğlu, for his precious contributions.

Cihangir Kavuncu
July 2017

Introduction

There are many works about human resources. These usually describe a theory or focus on a certain topic. Human resources is a working field where I believe it is hard to put theory into practice. External factors, administrative understanding, and perspective generally move human resources applications away from theory. Companies define human resources under their corporate structure as "secondary" or "other" management. Although this situation is different in some of the multinational companies, the common approach in the sector takes this direction. In this book, I prefer to examine human resources field integrally.

The fact that humans underpin an organization means that human resources will find a place for itself in a management structure that is only about "me" and employees are considered as "them." This is the most common situation in companies and countries. Because of companies that are not corporate enough and are managed by a "family business" mindset, human resources applications are not practiced as they have to be and are implemented arbitrarily and incompletely. Yet **human resources is a process combination that must be managed with an integration of modules.**

If you implement these modules incompletely, the process will be incomplete as well. In this respect, companies that have rendered their applications unmanageable and hard to resolve will keep these in use for years, and, in the end, their revision will be costly and time-consuming. Companies in such a system will not be able to figure out the source of the problem; they will even not be able to find the malfunctions.

Human resources is responsible for managing a complicated process in which it is hard to put theoretical information into practice. Because of the reasons mentioned above, human resources managers have difficulty deciding where to start and figuring out whether an idea is applicable. These troubles mainly result from not being able to manage the issue with a managerial approach as well as not being able to convince upper management. I believe that the main cause of this is thinking as a human resources manager rather than a manager of the organization.

You may ask what this means. Here it is what I mean: a human resources manager must think like a general manager. This perspective will provide a sense of ownership and a holistic and visionary logic to the human resources manager by asking the question, "What would I do if I were the general manager?" This mentality is fundamental for the success of the applications.

In addition, human resources managers must know how to speak with "business language." **"Human resources language" is perceived by the management to be a language that brings only extra cost to the company and never speaks about benefit.** Each case: must be analyzed by asking following questions "Why should we train? Why should we hire? For what should we pay more? How and when should we change?" The issue should be presented to management only if the answers are positive and convincing to HR. Projects and processes that are presented to the management without first finding these answers will not be accomplished. Human resources must remain on the right path and reach out to achieve the desired objectives in this way only on its long-term journey. There is no other method than that.

You should not read this book from the beginning till the end at once. It is more like a reference book that you can look at when you need it. For that reason, it should be read and understood when it is necessary. Should you have queries, feel free to tweet me at "@cihangir55."

1

Process and Relationship Management

HR is based on process and relationship, but relationship management without process takes HR to populism.

Thirty years ago, the human resources department was not prominent and generally performed its duties as a control department. But today, it is a recognized fact that human resources' role is not limited to a control department that manages costs. It also includes accomplishing healthy growth, ensuring sustainability, and, when necessary, influencing strategy. This recognition became more accurate after the economic crisis, which removed the advantage companies had of hiding inefficient operational costs behind product prices. In short, employee management became a topic companies needed to prioritize.

In the past, due to the importance of cost control, human resources activities were assigned to finance departments. This may not be a valid approach in most organizations as the formal structure, but informally in management's understanding, it is still recognized as described. When corporations manage human resources in this way, it is not easy to go from a controller mindset to a leader mindset. Human resources was supposed to provide strategy and control at the same time, besides controlling the cost. It is not only hiring and firing; rather, the real duty is to manage the organization's sustainability. This is the only way for an institution to learn about not only recording and calculating costs but also managing by systemic and sustainable infrastructure.

Sustainability goes with efficiency. This does not mean creating efficiency when it is needed but obtaining continuous efficiency management, leading to an adaptable and agile organizational mindset. Unless healthy growth management is ensured, companies will experience periods of excessive growth and excessive downsizing. Because of the tendency to invest and spend money during any growth process period, the risk of making a mistake is also high. Human resources should check whether the culture of growth is strong and well established. If it is not—meaning the question of "why" is not answered and growth plans are detached from each other due to lack of a common strategy—the system will pull down the desire for growth. I will not speak about this topic too much, since the number of the companies that perform actual strategic planning is low. However, if it is applied, human resources should definitely take a guiding role in the process.

A human resources manager seeking a long-term solution with an infrastructure configuration in its base should find the answers to the following questions:

- Does the company have a written personnel policy? Are the rights and the use of these rights defined and available in the system?
- Are operational processes defined and well known to employees?
- As a department, can human resources contribute to financial and managerial reporting?
- Does the human resources department really contribute to the managers' decision-making?
- Does the organizational structure depend on written rules, or is it done randomly?
- Is there any organizational succession plan that controls assignments?
- Are recruitment and development tasks managed in a process?
- Are wages and vested benefits under control and managed on a scale that reflects a value-added basis and respects organizational levels?
- Does the human resources manager attend the company's management board meetings?

If you answered negatively to most of these questions, it will be hard for you to perform human resources tasks in your company lest you appear "cute" to your upper manager, your employees, or other managers. The work you do will vary according to each person or department. It will be unclear what is right and what is wrong. Satisfaction will be temporary, and creating long-term policies will be hard. In the end, human resources will automatically become a registry and application center.

Therefore, creating human resources policies must be your choice. It is important to find out the department's reason for existing and to developing policies accordingly. For example, although human resources may have fundamentally the same reason for existing in a production company and in a corporation, its purpose varies according to company strategy. First, top management must be convinced about these policies and reasons. It is not only the general manager whom you need to convince. You also must convince the managers who occupy same level as you. In some organizations, it is even important to work with the informal general manager, who has a big influence on other managers and the organization. It is vital that the system accepts the change. Therefore, human resources should also understand the informal structure of the company to keep policies alive and active.

After identifying the basic human resources personnel management rules, ethical code, and discipline rules for at least three to four years, these rules should be applied without any exception to ensure compliance. However, health checks are important to see if there is a need for minor changes. To do that, human resources must work with the help of employees and managers. This can happen through workshops, info lines, or visits to and discussions with the employees. Once the base has been established, human resources policies should cover all the department's subprocesses. We can mainly sort these as follows:

- Recruitment
- Placement
- Performance
- Promotion and assignment
- Management of development activities
- Organizational management

- Wage and vested benefits management
- Regulations/ethical work and how to apply
- Travel type and expense management

These rules must always be used as a reference when the company acts on any human resources processes—without any exception, as said. The most important aspect of this is to have a strong human resources department that protects the rules and rejects any contrary applications. Even if the internal client is right in his or her discourses, the application must be kept and maintained as it is. The opposed position from the employees to aply the rules in their favor or management to manage as they wish so both benefits from their perspective individually. For sure, this is easier for employees and management, but it is a danger to the corporation. It is an attempt to change or stretch the rules instead of obeying them.

I had an interesting discussion in one of my jobs, just after I started working. Before my start, the human resources department was ranked lower than other departments, and it was used per their needs and how they wished at any stage of the process. After hearing about the title arrangement and the title of human resources, I said to the general manager, "It is clear what you are saying by keeping the human resources title at the bottom. You are saying, 'I don't care about this job.' If you want me and the company to be successful, you should give me the highest title that you can give. Otherwise, there is no need for me to be here. Another employee would be more helpful to you."

It was important to make people believe human resources is to be taken seriously, and that, this time, change is going to happen.

My next conversation with the general manager occurred two months later, during the salary increase period. One of the department managers was getting along well with the general manager. He always found a way to obtain privileges and keep his department's employees one step ahead and with extra benefits. It was an unfair situation, as we were not able to offer extra benefits for everyone. I said, "No, you have a limit, and that is the maximum increase we can make." We had an argument, but I persisted, and we ended our call without resolution.

The next day, when the general manager saw me, he told me, "We may offer something extra for that department."

Then I asked, "Would you like to keep this company as your company or make it a corporate one?"

This topic never came up again. After that, whenever this person wanted something extra, he came to the human resources department to ask for it. I acted tough in this case because it is important from the beginning to show that human resources is as important as other departments, and its contribution may be even higher. Later, this manager and I became friends.

2

Balance Is Hard Work

HR is the most unpopular department because it always touches the hygiene part of Maslow. Whereas motivators are possessed by managers. Keeping balance is hard work.

Research shows that human resources is one of the least popular departments in a company. This is because it deals mostly with matters which touch basic needs (such as physical needs, sense of belonging, and sense of security), ranked at the bottom of Maslow's hierarchy. Human resources departments' main duties—including recruitment, dismissal, salary, constitution of benefits, and performance management—are woven directly into employee pockets. It is unlikely that an employee and a manager will both have a positive perception of these needs. I have never experienced managers or employees saying their salaries or benefits are where they should be. They always benchmark against their peers or even their bosses and say, "If this guy is making this much, I have to make more." Increasing salary is not enough to change the perception of human resources. A company may have the best salary and benefit structure, but unless you support these by meeting employees' emotional and motivational needs, the perception of human resources will always be the same.

When you Google, "Why do we hate human resources?" you find more than 2,600,000 hits (as of 19/4/2018). This shows us that people have too many concerns about human resources. The human resources department should continuously ask itself, "How can we improve our perception?"

The first thing to do is to focus on the motivational factors of the Maslow hierarchy and try to create balance in a way that is fair and understood by all. The theory says that if a company does not treat physical, security, and belonging needs fairly, improvements on motivational factors—such as respect, recognition, and self-actualization—do not yield the explosive results. I believe this is not entirely true. My experience shows me that the way to reduce the negative impact of de-motivating factors is to recognize and keep open the path of empathy and respect.

Simply put, HR should touch the heart of the people by systematically helping them understand their potential and how much they are cared for. To do this, HR applications and processes should be customer focused (meaning employee focused) and also segmented per employee cluster—just like we segregate our customers.

Having a single process for a diversified population is a major issue in an environment where we have limited sources and different generations. Some very basic products we use include bonuses, sales incentives, overtime payment, and home office work, but these benefits are mostly regulated by law.

In one company I worked for, we came up with the idea to measure the effectiveness of our HR products—gauging whether they created value to the employee, company, or even the community. We decided to base our findings on Maslow's hierarchy theory. We prepared questions with a global survey company to understand where each employee placed himself or herself on the hierarchy. Then we took these questions and measured motivation and engagement using the same principles. The ultimate purpose, as mentioned, was to understand whether HR services was creating value for employees by touching the heart of the problem or whether time and energy were being wasted. The results were fascinating.

The first pilots we ran showed us that employees could be grouped into four clusters:

Locomotive: These employees are the most satisfied and ready to go. They are happy to work in the company, friendly to the environment, and high achievers. We called them locomotives, or drivers of performance. They were not necessarily high but they were surely top-level performers. They marked Maslow motivators such as career development and involvement in projects as the most important areas. Salary was not mentioned as a top-level issue. You can see in the table that they are positioned in the upper-right cluster. "Satisfaction" and "willingness" among these employees were determined as high.

Potential: Employees falling into this area have the willingness and enthusiasm to be part of the company. However, their level of satisfaction is low due to several reasons. They are either doing the wrong job, their superior may be creating an environment that is not suitable for them, or there may be other similar reasons. Because of this, they tend to list "hygiene" factors as motivators—level of salary, benefits, physical work environment, etc. In a nutshell, their level of satisfaction is low, but their willingness is high. These employees should be considered offered different programs to lead them towards the locomotive cluster.

Indecisive: These employees haven't decided how to feel about the company. Accordingly, they cannot clearly define their expectations from the company. They are satisfied with the things they possess and somehow perform fairly. They do things they are told to do. However, their hunger to do more is low; therefore they fail to engage with the team, the work, or the company. Special programs are needed to lead them toward a motivating environment, namely the locomotive cluster. In short, they are satisfied, but their willingness is low.

Potential		Locomotive	
	Level of Satisfaction ↓		Level of Satisfaction ↑
Low		High	
	Willingness ↑ High		Willingness ↑ High
	Employees		Employees
Hostage		**Indecisive**	
	Level of Satisfaction ↓		Level of Satisfaction
Low		↑High	
	Willingness ↓ Low		Willingness ↓ Low
	Employees		Employees

Hostage: They are not satisfied with the company. They might even be against the company. They do not want to do more, and would often even do less if possible. In addition, they influence high performers' condition negatively and pull them down. On the other hand, these employees marked "job security" as their top need and are happy to have it. They marked "salary," "vested benefits," and similar hygiene factors ahead of all other aspects as problematic areas. They were happy with job security but complained about salary and benefits. Obviously, their performance level was very low.

This type of employee exists in all organizations. As we know, the performance systems we use in HR do not always reflect reality. So how do they survive? Basically, we do so by building a very close relationship to our superiors, helping the boss with their individual needs and hiding in teams, acting as if we are performing and performing support actions that keep them going until retirement. Hostages are the real problem for companies who wish to reach a better level of performance and engagement.

As a result of our study, we found that when human resources products are monotype, it becomes impossible to track the real impact to the employee. In other words, when we do employee satisfaction surveys, we ask generic questions to our employees, such as

'I am happy to be a part of this team?'

Then we asked the employee to mark a "true or false" scale of "1 to 5." When we get the results, we first look into the general ratio, if the overall results are fine, then the general trend is not to apply any specific program. We may implement some program to maintain it, but likely we don't even know what it means to maintain that level. Some further departmental analysis is also performed to see if employees in that department or unit are okay.

If the results are generally "not okay," then we design programs that we hope will produce a turnaround. It does not work. I have applied so many programs this way, but it is not the right way to do it. Why? Because we are not focusing on the individual needs of the employees. We are focusing on the department- or unit-based needs of the organization.

Therefore, programs designed to serve all do not work. They are a waste of money and time.

Being in balance means meeting the specific needs of your employee with focused products—just as we do for our customers in a segmented matter. If a company has 70 percent engagement as a result of a satisfaction survey, that means there are people who marked higher than 70 and some who marked lower than 70. An average is not going to help HR. HR does not have much chance to influence the hostages since they will be resisting change because of their fear of losing their job. Programs should focus more on those who have potential and those who are indecisive about moving up, and they should support locomotives. HR should make people work in projects, encourage them with a good career plan for their future, and put processes or programs into place that increase self-confidence and commitment to the company.

If HR applies such programs successfully, the negative perception of human resources will fade away since needs are being met better than before. If we can't enact programs that appeal to employees at the top rung of the hierarchy, hygiene factors will become more disturbing and make employees feel uncomfortable.

Another important issue is to ensure balance with the line manager. If we can put across our applications to line managers clearly and involve them in the process, the work of human resources will automatically be much easier.

Human resources should always work with line managers while designing a program and come to an agreement on the aspects of the project. This way, human resources will share the risk of both failure and success. Human resources should ask managers to work, communicate, and explain to their employees what is going to happen; if not, they should stand by HR while it explains the project or the situation. This should be the way to manage, it and it should be embedded in the company culture. Human resources should always be in the intermediary position. A successful HR usually acts as an intermediator or provider to the system rather than a power center that regulates the environment. That comes with more involvement of line managers, by including them more in process. This approach gives HR a greater role as part of the business.

3

Generalist HR versus Business Partner

The "business partner" period is over; nowadays there is a more general HR. The reason is not the decrease in detail but rather cost pressure.

The human resources' function " was basically giving needed services as they were personnel department in the past so department just was fulfilling the expected by management, not giving a direction to human resources management of the companies.

In some companies, the expectation from HR was mainly limited to hiring, training, preparing payroll processes, and dismissing. Even training activities were not defined as a human resources functions. It proceeded this way until approximately the 1980s.

We started to see "human resources" as a title in the 90s, but the real function was still typically personnel management. HR was heard mainly with the large organizations doing business internationally with a multinational base. In later years, towards the end of the 90s, it began to work in a way that befit its name.

However, it was still not strategic, reactive, and controlling function. There were several types of research on human resources as well as geographically different understandings, but in 1996, when Dave Ulrich proposed a new way of servicing the client in his famous book *HR Champions*, he started a trend in westernized companies to introduce "HR business partnership." We believed this was the gateway to better customer service. This period was the start of two main aspects of HR service level. One was the "expertise center," which mainly consisted of compensation and benefits, training, administration, and other similar areas. The other was the business partnership, which was mainly related to the customer. We hoped that by having business partner in place, HR would be close to the business, providing more help to line managers.

The suggestion of HR business prtner was based on the idea that human resources should work as follows:

Business unit consultants: These should mainly be in contact with customers, intertwined with those who are experienced in career, performance, and development, even in some companies HR business partners report into business line management.

Excellence center: This center serves business consultants by doing all kinds of work within the substructure or within the process, thus increasing the quality of service given to the customer. Even payroll and personnel affairs were becoming out-serving work.

Education: Human resources professionals in this field act together with other HR professionals (consultants to business unit), and they ensure employee development.

This idea really changed the understanding of HR in the manager's daily activities. It has resulted in more internal customer satisfaction and in human resources applications that are based on specialization and improvement of customer service quality. They also enable the team to provide faster service to customers. Business units felt human resources was closer and started to involve this department in their works.

I believe those good days are over. My reasoning is based on several facts. Human resources was not able to create an "end-to-end" system that allows HRBP to act as the salesperson to the customer. We faced issues of not responding on time and being reactive to the changes. Expertise centers started to pile up, relying on excessive head counts to serve better, and that increased the cost of the service. It even put line managers out of the loop, and HRBP became too close to the business. The consequences of this were as follows:

1. The relation of HRBP started to be functional at the highest level of any department. They preferred to talk to SVPs or other similar

levels. Since there were very limited self-services introduced to the line managers on other levels to get the job done, it became important to agree with the head of the department.

2. HRBPs became very close to the business. I have seen some cases in the past where HRBP were the ones asking HR to bend the rules to not harm their relationship with the head of the department. Processes started to dilute and differ from one department to another, which also affected the level of service, and internal customers started to bypass regulations with ease. Therefore, trust became an issue between the internal customer and human resources.

3. The role of line manager in the HR process became unclear. HR started to manage simple things in complex ways. The line manager was not able to understand the rules. How to promote employees? How to discharge a person? What to do if an employee wants to join a training program? It all became a matter of talking to the HRBP and if not then to expertise center people. This service model required HR to increase number of employee so that we can serve better to the business line and to the employee.

4. Within HR, end-to-end process style was lost, resulting in silo-ing. HR managers became enemies even of themselves, fighting each other to get things done. That really broke team spirit.

As a reaction to these developments, management started to question the cost of HR. It was not at a healthy level. At this point, we started outsourcing our expertise centers to other companies, hoping that costs would decrease and service would improve. At the beginning, costs went down, for sure, but service level definitely deteriorated. Because we asked our employees to call a center to solve their issues, in some cases, we needed to create service centers for employees of multiple countries. In addition, human resources lost its flexibility.

I think the first solution to all these issues is to expand the knowledge level of each employee in the HR department with a penetrated approach. Today, if I talk to a BP, he or she knows very well what is going on with the internal client but has limited knowledge of expertise center topics, or vice versa.

We had the same issue in a bank that I used to work for. BPs were overly controlled by expertise center employees on the service side. What we did was to launch a training program for all employees within a curriculum and create certificate programs to support and encourage their learning. Depending on their jobs, we segmented our programs into two:

Common modules that were mandatory for certain jobs. Some examples include HR Planning Recruitment, Career Management, Position and Compensation Management, Labor Law, HR Metrics and Measurement Tools, HR and Social Media, Preparing Effective PowerPoint Presentations, and Train the Trainer.

Superior and manager modules which were mandatory for this level included Managerial Skills, Feedback for Coaches, Macroeconomic Indicators, General Credit and Risk Notion, Organizational Behavior, Consultancy Skills, Change Management, and Communication and HR Branding.

We included a qualification exam in the program, to be made after each training activity, as well as a certificate to ensure graduation. The program was very successful at disseminating information among all colleagues and increasing the service level to the internal customer. Afterward, when HR went to a customer, they felt stronger.

This approach also helped HR decrease the number of employees and improve ratios. All this kept HR on the cutting edge of efficiency and effectiveness. A growing department in good times should always plan to work effectively rather than reduce staff in bad times.

A second but equally necessary solution is to have an "end-to-end" system in place. Otherwise, it is not possible to achieve effective HR. You may improve the efficiency ratio by cutting h/c but, since we intent to not change the processes HR department may even worsen the numbers compared to the original starting point.

We were able to improve our ratio only after we decided to put a system in place. To ensure an efficient process, we had to automate as much as possible, using line managers through the self-services and ask them to involve more in the HR decision-making process. This way, our employee ratio improved from 50 to between 110 and 120 per HR in three to four years. We will discuss this topic in more depth when we discuss cost management.

In my opinion, the substructure of the human resources department is based on the fact that they work only with manpower without a strong structure. Customer focus can be improved only with an integrated system and well-cultivated HR personnel at all levels. This requires creating an efficient learning environment. A human resources department with extra employees shouldn't create satisfaction; in contrast, this will result in less service to the customer.

4

Who Makes People Happy, HR or Managers?

A manager makes an employee happy, not HR. The duty of human resources to make the manager act as HR and not to make itself a power center.

Human resources is perceived as a department that needs to manage "humans" on behalf of the company. Due to this perception, HR employees always find themselves dealing with problems. Whenever there is an issue in a process or programs, even in relations caused by managers, human resources end up handling it as if it were their issue. In fact, the first responsibility belongs to line managers when issues of compensation and benefits, talent, and development are raised. Human resources must establish systems that allow managers do their job themselves, rather than doing all these on their behalf.

Some HR managers might think that having this kind of power makes human resources a point of reference and brings more power in the management. Human resources want to have the last word so they can be asked, act, and decide. Statements such as "HR can send him to this training [or that training]," "the performance of this person should be [like this]," and "that employee can move to another job" makes human resources more powerful. I support administrative control for weak companies, but ultimately human resources become a police department. When I refer to power, I mean a system's structural and organizational efficiency.

When I joined the bank, it was HR's duty to prepare the list of people eligible for promotion. The list was prepared with limited cooperation of line managers. This meant that the manager had limited authority; he or she could participate in the decision-making process to the degree that HR allowed. As a result, human resources had more control than necessary. Of course, human resources should provide data on performance, disciplinary measures, and demographics, but this list was prepared by HR only, and promotion time was set for two times a year. This meant removing responsibility completely from the relevant management and giving it to human resources. In this case, the human resources department took full responsibility so the line manager did not feel any accountability for the assignment. They would often come back for changes, saying things like, "Yes [this person] is a good performer, but I don't want her promoted now." HR's reply was usually not much help since the file created was already a defined one. Employees were also following the developments, estimating that they should be promoted. Therefore, it was given that the employee would be promoted. On the other hand, line managers were under pressure to change HR's decision. This was not a healthy process.

We created a different process to solve this issue. In the beginning, we had meetings with line managers to set up the system together. The basic outcomes were as follows:

- We canceled the fixed promotion calendar and changed it to a flexible one. This allowed managers act whenever they want (faster if needed). This has also changed the perception of the line manager in the eyes of the employee.
- We told the line managers that employees were their staff and HR would only provide them data about the employee and ask the manager to make the decision at promotion time.
- HR stepped back from the controller role and moved towards a provider role, leaving more space to the line managers.

We basically said, "Managers may give a promotion anytime; human resources provides control only in terms of rules." If the process is right, the decision is the manager's! We launched this with a communication campaign to keep all concerned parties informed of the change.

Of course, backing up these changes with a system is very important.

After we launched the program, we stood by and trained the managers, making them comfortable with the new approach and system. Line manager should clearly understand what it means to evaluate performance—why giving feedback is important and how to do it, why we identify high potentials and develop them for the future of the company. This helps the manager become more involved in the process and also increases the sense of ownership.

By educating managers, HR enables them understand that it is part of their job to keep performance high, and doing HR tasks is a part of their job. If this is not the path HR chooses, then human resources—as previously stated—will continue to work as a police department, which mainly talks about things that cannot be done.

However, duty sharing should be balanced. In some companies, the responsibility is given fully to managers, by telling them, "The employee is under your responsibility." In these companies, it is important to have a common approach to the main HR processes that a company should have. Generally, the main HR processes, such as hiring, compensation, and performance management, are done by managers at the basic level. If a system is not in place, this approach will be dangerous for the future of the company since the actions will differ from manager to manager and will not be based on a common approach.

Ideal human resources management is undertaken with shared responsibility between human resources and managers. This way, the company will be able to put the employee at the heart and also make processes corporate. Human resources applications can be made uniform by setting up infrastructure and putting in place a system based on the strategic view of the company. Then the manager holds the operational responsibility and becomes an enabler of the system. This is the first duty of any human resources department.

The other important task is to maintain cost management within the department. In some, even major companies, cost is managed by the CFO or some similar field. If HR does not have the budget, then cost management will not be sustainable; HR will be told what to do in their projects and processes and be told how to manage them. It is therefore essential that HR maintain cost management.

The most proactive management style in cost management is structuring organizational costs. To ensure this, company structure should be regulated with strict rules and regulations to control promotions and staffing at a healthy level. If not, then organizations extend more than needed in the growing environment, costs increased, and after certain period, they become unmanageable. Next, the company ends up un-employing people, at high cost, in the hope that operational costs will decrease. This is rarely the case, since companies do not intend to manage such h/c savings through process simplification. Therefore, after a while, the company ends up with a higher h/c and cost.

Organizational management should build company structure based on job evaluation or similar systems. Therefore, the job should be the center for all HR activities, such as recruitment, compensation, benefits, promotions, bonus pay, development, and succession planning. Employees should be activated only if there is a job in the system; if not, then the existence of that employee should be questioned. **HR should not—I repeat, should not—base its organizational activities on the employee assignment, organizational desing should be based on the job itself. Otherwise, it will be so impossible to control costs and manage a healthy company.**

Another way of managing HR cost is to allocate costs to related departments and ask managers to be liable for their results. In this manner, the manager will know that if the company will not manage HR costs wisely, especially in services business, sustainability will not be possible. For this, a well-working financial MIS system is a must. In addition, monitoring should be embedded in financial targets and results of managers to create accountability among the managers.

Labor turnover rate is normally a goal of the company, but it is usually perceived as an HR department goal. In fact, the line manager is the one who creates labor turnover. Employees are hired for the company, but the manager has a great influence on employee performance and engagement. If the manager is good, then the company is second in the employee's mind. The employee first believes in the manager, and secondly they consider the company culture and treatment. It is not so wrong to say that people leave for reasons related to their manager, not related to the company. However, if human resources does not set up systems that make the manager's life easier, than the increased turnover is HR's fault. HR should prepare programs to make life easier for managers with respect to engagement, performance, and other aspects. These programs should be defined and designed together with business units. Only in this way can work responsibility be equally distributed between manager and human resources so that the employee will have a balanced perception of company and manager.

5

Ethics Is the Most Important Regulator

An ethical company should have an ethics code and corporate governance, which is the foundation of the company. HR is the most important organ to achieve it.

Firstly, we should ask ourselves, "Why is ethics important?" Ethics sets the rules and framework for the things we plan and execute. It outlines what we should not do. As an example, you can specify that people are not allowed to talk about race and religion. When we set up this as a rule, we need to make sure that managers and employees reach the same level of knowledge by training and education. By doing so, we regulate and control the behavior.

There are some units that control ethics in large companies. For example, compliance offices in banks control ethics codes by law, but in most others, HR acts as a compliance office to fulfill this duty. To achieve this, HR should work on two main documents, namely personnel management guidance and ethics codes.

Personnel management guidance should be the reference book to check what should be done and what is available to any employee on any level. On the other hand, the ethics code is a document that will help the employee understand how work life is regulated in a broader sense, focused more on regulations. If a company misses either of these, "the right thing" to do differs from one manager or employee to another.

Someone will see information sharing with a customer as normal, while others will find this dangerous. At the beginning of my career, I joined a company. At our first day of orientation, we got the rules of ethics and how important it was to apply the rules. The company stated that the *important thing is not what you do but also how you do it.*

It is a fact that an ethics code increases team spirit and eliminates the sense of "self." Thus it helps to move forwards towards institutionalization. By institutionalization, we mean the creation of a corporate culture through a single type of conduct described for all. We have said that the ethics code defines what shouldn't be done. Therefore, the question "How do we express what needs to be done?" comes to mind. Three separate corporate documents must support the ethics document to determine what should be done and what the right behavior is. These important documents are Corporate Governance, Human Resources Governance, and Communication Governance.

Ethics codes should be based on the facts of corporate governance or a constitution. It is common to have ethics codes but not written governance. In any case, ethics codes are found in the reference to common values. When you create a system based on governance and ethics, it will provide more commitment to the company.

Does a company without any ethics code fail? Of course not, but with regulations such as ethics codes, a company ensures the continuation of performance and also helps maintain the positive perception of the company. Therefore, the company becomes sustainable. When you don't set ethics codes, you don't describe the way to reach sustainable success. How will the employee behave while working? What is the right way? Being successful by treading on employees' toes? Obtaining knowledge by stealing or copying? What should the behavior be toward the client? If the company leaves this decision to the interpretation of the employee, this is not sustainable. Each employee's adoption of an individual behavior for a common approach makes inter-company behaviors serve for a shared future and increases the understanding of what the company is for.

Therefore, our behavioral actions must be based on a structured, well-understood, and top-down practiced governance!

6

Be Fair to the Employee

Being fair to the employee doesn't mean treating all employees the same way. It means treating all employees at the same level, rank, or segment equally.

The concept of fairness has become prominent in this generation. Previously, companies facing this issue would manage the "perception of fairness" rather than the problem itself. With the new generation, companies are expected to create solution to fairness issues. Employees care not only that they are treated fairly by the company, but they also care that others are treated fairly.

Fairness differs from one culture to another. For example, the culture in the more performance-oriented companies is different from that in hierarchical and seniority-based companies. A fair environment, which is expected in seniority-based companies, is one that ensures an equal treatment of employees at the same level. In performance-oriented companies, the fairness of the performance process is questioned within the concept of performance measurement.

Fairness does not mean equal treatment. Companies should create systems and infrastructures that allow both employee and employer to act fairly, or at least control the culture and daily operation fairly so that they can create a fair environment. For example, if there is a performance system, the company should create equal opportunities for everyone in the performance system. If there is a balanced distribution in goals between employees and their evaluation is made clear and understandable, then there is monotony, which results in fairness. This means that the system is working correctly. Apart from this, promotions are critical to the concept of fairness in human resources. In many companies, promotions are usually based on observation and monitoring of managers instead of corporate systems. Even employees get used the system by saying, "My future is between my manager's two lips—whether he says yes or no." This is a problem that affects the notion of fairness. For this reason, the most important thing human resources must do is to be transparent in systems and processes so that working conditions become self-monitoring. They have to explain clearly by saying, "We use these criteria for promotion, and the manager is one of the decision-makers for the evaluation process. In fact, he is *the* decision maker." Merely establishing authorized signatures list and counting this a completion of a duty leads human resources to reach deceptive results and it leads structural disruption due to uncontrollable discourse. Human resources have to be in connection with employee. Only in this way can it build confidence and improve the perception of the system.

The company should certify fairness by continuously practicing it in its processes. People believe there is a fair environment only when the company delivers what it has promised and when employees experience what is said in their daily wotk life. I would like to give an example from my own experience.

In a bank with a large branch network, it was critical to create an environment where branch managers were selected fairly where the system was transparent to candidates. It was also important for the bank, since revenues were generated by the network of the bank. Therefore, human resources had to put a system in place to select the best candidate in a fair manner. This way, the ones who were not selected would believe in the selection's fairness and keep performing at the highest level possible. In the beginning, the perception was that region managers were the ones who played the key role in the appointment process. Therefore, candidates perceived their candidacy totally relied on region manager's wish. Although the process of human resources did not allow region managers to act as the main driver, confidence in the process could not be built. The potential assignment list was prepared according to performance and other similar criteria, people were nominated to the branches based on a ranking list for open positions, and the branch manager was selected from the list within a given rule set. Ultimately, the decision was taken with the regional manager and business management, but there was discomfort. It reached such a level of distrust that even the results of the assessment were questioned by unsuccessful candidates. We often heard comments like, "I would like to see how I was marked on my results" and "I don't believe this." To ameliorate this, we involved possible candidates in designing a better process. We conducted workshops and included employees, branch managers, and regional managers in the process, and we changed the process as per their requests.

The new approach was based on open communication and was very transparent. We put together an assessment center that had 30–35 percent weight in the total evaluation matrix. We declared that any employee in the network meeting certain criteria could go through the simulated assessment, which was a branch manager post. In this way we could evaluate the performance of a candidate for a simulated branch manager role. We also added factors in the selection criteria, such as performance, mobility, and level of education (high school or college), and we evaluated them with a percentage rate. Candidates even evaluated themselves to see if they were suitable for application to the simulation. The candidates could see their rank and their score. Afterward we invited them to a group interview. Two regional managers, human resources managers, and top managers also participated in the interview, selected according to their most recent evaluation. The other important aspect was to ask them to apply freely to the announced positions and see their application's ranking for that position.

After applying this system for two to three years without exceptions, employees started to believe in the fairness of the system. The key was to involve them in the selection process design and make it transparent to all who applied. Of course, effective communication became an indispensable part of it. Therefore, we can conclude that fairness can only be established through

1) **Clearness:** Employees want to know what they have to do, and how, to reach results for example: "Will I take an exam?" "Will I be evaluated?" "Who will decide?" "Who has the last word in decision-making process?"

2) **Sustainability**: HR should apply the same system over and over. There may be exceptions, but these should be explained and understood. We sometimes had areas when we not receive any applications from the selected pool of candidates; then we announced them openly to regional people and selected among those. This was also a transparently managed process. It is essential to build trust in the system.

3) **Criteria**: The set of criteria that any candidate must meet should be clear and understood. The employee should see them so that she can decide her own path.

4) **The right to select:** At the end of the process, candidates who were successful should be able to select where they prefer to work. In regional banking, business conditions and the quality of the branch are important factors for success. Therefore, the company should allow candidates to apply to the branches they like. This improves the sense of ownership and performance. At the end, the regional manager had a right to assign someone from three or four candidates who had high scores. If their selection was not the first one in the ranking, they were supposed to give a very good reason why they did not select the first one.

Another important topic that defines whether the system is fair is performance targeting and evaluation systems. Performance systems are usually perceived as unfair processes by employees. Even though performance evaluation systems are connected to a target card, employees do not see them as fair systems. The target card company set should be clear, sustainable, and understood, and the performer should have a say in it. The target card shows what a person must perform to reach the target. It should be regulated by the company, of course, but a bottom-up approach would add meaning and increase the sense of ownership of one's performance. If the person reaches the target, he should be able to see it clearly. Fairness is also affected by "how the employee reaches the target." The employee should be controlled by another section of the performance card to evaluate if "how" is in the frame of company culture, how defines and reviews if employee is acting within the given rules and cultural frame of the company while they perform.

In conclusion, fairness alone doesn't mean anything. The system should move towards creating a fair environment with all its elements. It can be a long and tough road. Human resources have duty here as well, but most important is for management to have sufficient knowledge and willingness to explain why some are treated differently. It is not because "HR said so" or because "That's just the way it is." Management should take a stand and explain that it is because employee did not perform well that he would not be capable of holding that position. If this is not the culture, human resources' duty is difficult and HR will suffer. Employees keep track of the actions of a company, not its words. Once trust is lost, fairness dies, and it is very costly to get it back.

Unfortunately, it is not enough for human resources or the general manager to believe in this; the entire system is supposed to follow. Human resources must explain to top management and other managers the reason that company should be so strict about the "walk-to-talk" principle. That is the only way to create a culture.

7

High or Missed Potential

Career and development should be sequential. Employees who succeed in the early years of their career show lower performance over the years due to development gap. They tend to not take risks. Therefore, if a high-potential employee isn't managed well, he becomes a missed potential.

High-potential (or talent) management is an area on which companies spend a lot of time, money, and effort. There are conferences around the globe and jobs that employ only high potentials. Every year, in most companies, we spend much time discussing how to hire, develop, and please these employees so they stay with us.

What is potential management? Why do we manage potentials separately?

"Potential" is a set of skills a person has that may bring significant advantage compared to others. We assume that this potential will turn into higher performance and development level so that one can grow faster than others.

Potentials are quick in understanding, faster in thinking, better in acting, more result oriented, and better able to manage people better than others. We are looking for people who are "corporate Wonder Woman or Batman," who can save us from disasters and unmet deadlines and give us hope that the future is bright and hopeful. This is a very hard track, and I also believe that it harms the company culture. I believe in talent, of course, but not in the sense of how we treat employees.

Let's say there is a population of a thousand employees. As there are people who show high performance, there are also high-potential employees who can really work at a top position. However, the way we determine those employees is very important. Is there a systematic method in which top- or mid-level managers determine high-potential employees in the company? Or does the company employ the traditional method, which I call "corridor management," which puts forward the employee who is closest to the managers? In case there is no infrastructure for determining the skill and abilities of employees, many employees with greater potential are likely to be overlooked except for those determined by "corridor management." Normally, we expect to see around 10 percent of high potential in a population. This rate can increase to 15 percent under various circumstances, even higher in some cases.

Managers generally confuse high-potential with high-performing. They slog on their prior decision and generally they put the employee forward who has high performance. Potential and performance are complementary but different aspects of the employee. Evaluating potential is a difficult process. There are many ways to measure it—personality tests, behavioral tests (via assessment centers), cultural tests (made during recruiting)—but the main point is that if you cannot manage well after you recruit such energy or discover it, the generated potential become incapable. Why? Because potential energy remains potential energy until it is acted upon. According to the laws of physics, unless you convert potential energy to kinetic energy, it remains only potential. It is the same in management. I have seen people refer to as potentials who never took any risk in their life to show that they can also perform. I have seen people picked as potentials and treated as such but never raising their level of performance. I have seen managers who stick to their potentials and mark them as high achievers because they don't want to be perceived as lousy decision-makers.

Rapid promotion of a talented employee creates a ruined employee. They remain more attached to their more to their manager who asked for the promotion than they do to the company. This is also valid for the manager. The manager also feels very attached to the potential and thinks that without her, he will not be able to deliver results or be successful. We've all heard managers say, "If we don't give this promotion, s/he will go" or "We don't want to lose her." In this way the manager is declaring that he cannot manage potential properly. If human resources don't react to the needs of the manager, then it is to be blamed for the results and to be held responsible if the employee leaves the company.

Whenever an employee or manager comes to my room stating that he or she will leave the company for any reason, I just simply say, "It is okay. You may go." In most cases, they don't. I believe once they decide to go, paying them more so that they stay does not make them loyal employees. It just defers the decision.

Of course, the company will do fast tracks to test the potential for performance, but it should have rules to manage it. In a bank I worked for, we had a rule: when we assigned a high potential to another position, usually a higher one, we took him out of our first-priority high-potential list to see if he would be a potential again. This meant that the employee needed to perform and show the system that his potential had resulted in value creation.

There is no one right system. However, what we say and do are very important. It is very common to use 9-box grid to identify potential compared to the performance level of the employee. It is important how we define the boxes and make use of them. Supposing that human resources employs the right systems, at the top box, we should see the 10 percent highest-potential employees. Managers should then start putting them up as candidates for projects, jobs, etc. Human resources should be the ones to provide the system to the company to enable managers to make the right personnel decisions. Managers should be convinced that their performance is sustainable and adds value regardless of their work in projects or in various positions. This test must last at least one year. At that time, the employee should be forced and must learn success or failure. If this is not done correctly, high-potential employees will not continue to be high performers and remain successful at their positions.

Another important case is the recruitment of high-potential people and the management of their adaption to the company. A potential hired from outside is hired because of her success in another culture or environment. It is not easy for her to show the same performance in a new environment. She either adapts or leaves the company. There are many employees who started their job with great dreams but left after a short period. Recruitment paid little attention in HR. We usually intend to "fill" the positions. We do not have time to look for the right candidate since the business is pushing to fill the vacancy as soon as possible. Guess what they also ask HR to do—to recruit the best! This means they are looking for a person who was very successful in their other company and also has potential. Human resources should hire for a "cultural fit" first, then to look for potential and other matters. If the attitude is not what you are looking for, then the rest will not work.

High-potential management requires a patient process. When we promote or recruit, the most important thing is to be patient in high-potential management. Let me explain with an example. Suppose there is a manager who is very talented, who performs well, and who everyone likes. We promote her to an upper position because she is a potential and we don't want to lose her. We act fast, and after one year, we ask for her promotion to the level of director. Because it is an early promotion, the employee feels pressure to be successful in a short time to show that she can do it. Because this increases her stress too much, she loses her performance track and begins to panic. What usually happens next is that such employees go back to their comfort zone and try to do what they are good at. This is probably not what the company is asking for, but she continues the behavior, hoping it will bring performance and recognition. In reality, she is merely doing things required by her earlier assignment. She continues doing the same technical work that brought success in her prior position instead of making more decisions, managing more people, and evaluating more performance. Because she fears that asking about the things she does not know equates to losing time, she prefers to go to seminars to learn instead of consulting with subortunates or peers. That is shame and a sin in management. She thinks she does not need anyone to remind her of her development and says to herself, "I have the potential. Everyone likes me. I shouldn't lose this attention. I have to be successful. I shouldn't be put into trouble." But this approach does not prevent the lost of performance then, in short order, she moves on to another job to try again. This is a death cycle for the company. Getting experience is very important for a high-potential person. If it doesn't happen, human resources should manage the person's adaption process by suggesting coaching and development to assist. HR can also use an internal corporate consultant (buddy system) to guide them.

So far we have mentioned the things that human resources mainly should manage. Let's focus shortly on what managers should do to have better potential management:

1. While revealing high potentials, they should use HR tools and value them. For example, after a possible potential fails in the assessment results, managers often go against the system and say, "She is a high potential and loved by everyone." They insist that the process evaluates wrongly and causes inefficient results. On the other hand, we know that real potential doesn't mean being the closest person to a manager or having a good relationship with him. Real potential can be found in an undiscovered person. The manager should stick to the rule and try to improve the decision-making process. He should not create other methods of selection by pressurizing the system when he faces an unfavorable decision.

2. Managers should create situations for the potential to test his knowledge and increase his experience. You can put him in a difficult position to see if s/he can adjust to it and still perform. One simple example: A manager asks a potential to prepare a presentation. The decision is made that the manager will present it. But just before the presentation, without a prior notification, the manager asks the employee to present it. The potential's response to this request always tells the manager a story about the person as well as teaching the potential how to act in difficult situations. After the presentation, a feedback session helps the potential understand steps for future.

3. High-potential employees aren't managers' portieres. On the contrary, a high-potential employee is a person who stands somewhat apart from manager and knows how to create ideas against the manager. The manager must understand and allow this misalignment. The manager needs to be a little more patient when evaluating the high-potential employee. Demanding that everything happen immediately makes us reach for the wrong results. When a potential manager becomes a director, s/he start thinking of next setps very soon, questioning where s/he will go in two years; s/he wants to take the promotion immediately. In

order to make the best of a new position, the career process must be explained in detail. Generally, high-potential employees have long years in front of them but a progressively shorter career path. The manager should take her or his time to explain this patiently to the potential, make her or him feel and understood, and ensure that this is the best way to reach a sustainable level of performance.

4. Another important application for skill development is cross-assignment (cross-move). This means that a manager can make an employee change her department, promote her, and then take her back again. However, this requires a long learning process. Cross-move is very educational, but at the same time, it should be very well managed by human resources.

Generally, managers think high-potential development is a duty of human resources. However, it is fully the manager's duty to develop people and help them grow within the company. Human resources should provide the right systems and tools to help managers achieve such growth.

8

Customer Focus

The target of low costs in human resources is the enemy of customer focus. In this case, the best thing to do is to improve the infrastructure and the systems.

In the area of human resources, companies intend to keep their investment at a minimum. This is the result of cost pressure but is born of a shortsighted mindset. Any company that is successful and sustainable in its growth and revenues has based its journey on a balanced human resources and business management. Companies generally set financial goals in their long-term planning, and they plan to reach these goals without thinking about necessary employee investment. Therefore, they try to manage human resources while working with minimum possible costs. If the company continuously keeps human resource investments under cost pressure, it will begin to defuse itself, and HR will focus only on controlling the cost. When the number of HR employees is greatly diminished, if the infrastructure isn't strong enough, we also see a diminishing services and confusion of human resources structure. This leads to an environment in which HR becomes a shadow CFO, a financial center rather than a function that balances its own needs with efficient cost management. As a result, employees lack both behavioral and infrastructural practices.

Another reason for cost control in HR is the perception of HR by management. Management mostly see human resources as less important than sales, manufacturing, or business line of service, depending on the industry company functions. In the service sector, the perception differs in favor of HR. In service businesses such as finance, hotels, or other business in which the product is "human," training employees, recruiting correctly, and managing careers effective is just as important as generating the product for any manufacturing company. There is no product that you can see on a shelf or that you may market to make your sales easy. In a service business, the famous phrase of 4P (product, price, promotion, and place) becomes

Right Professional, Right Payment, Right Position, Right Promotion

Every success depends on who you recruit or promote, as well as people management.

In a bank that I worked for we, were training line managers on the aspects of human resources in daily life—how to use them, facts, etc. During our training, I always asked the question, "What is our product?" The replies focused on the financial products, such as deposits, loans, derivatives, etc. My question was a provocative one, to make them think differently. I replied that the main product was "human," and they were surprised, because they had not thought of humans as our main product. I continued with my striking the questioning: "Have you seen a half-full beverage bottle or detergent box or any similar product on the shelf?" They all agreed they had never seen this before. Then my following question was "Then why don't you let your employees go to the necessary training to learn so they can be ready for the customer?" At first, they did not understand what I was saying, but when I commented, "All the financial products you mention are the bundles you put around as promotional subproducts around your main product. If the main product is not at its best, the rest falls apart."

We can use the same logic for governments. "What is the main product of any government?" It is obviously the people we have in a country. That is why it is so important to have a sustainable and current education policy, based on long-term trends. This is because government is also in the service business. That is going to drive the future of the company or the government.

In most banks and companies, humans are not seen as the main focus. Management chooses to focus on the bottom line, revenues, and outside customers. Since doing business with large margins is not possible anymore, creating efficiency on costs and services is the key to success. The system requires management to think in the short term—three months, one year, and even every month in some businesses. All these reasons push them away from the reality that the employee is the first customer and that we need to take care of the employees to make it happen.

Then the main question is "How is human resources going to balance cost efficiency with human investment needs?" Considering that the expenditures are always limited, the infrastructure of human resources should be set up very well to ensure good management of these issues. When the infrastructure does not provide solutions to efficiency, the results of HR practices do not lead to desired outcomes. We go into the trap of un-employing people, hoping that it will save us. Nine out of ten times this means more h/c in the future, unless the company transforms its processes into an efficient human resources service level.

This is the only way we can balance efficiency with higher customer service.

In the absence of a strong infrastructure and too much focus on cost efficiency, human resources function turns into a management of processes. Practices will not lead to engagement and employees will not be happy with the services HR provides.

While implementing a good infrastructure in the HR system, the company should introduce a higher level of line manager involvement in the HR processes. In this way, managers can decrease their requests of reports and daily operational activities from the HR department, and more time can be spent on planning and strategic topics.

If there is no end-to-end system and the company decides to focus more on the internal customer, then this indicates a need to increase the headcount in HR. There is a very common ratio used for HR's efficiency:

Total number of employees in the company divided by total number of HR h/c

As previously mentioned, this ratio basically tells how many employees are served per HR h/c. It may be a discussion point to include/exclude administrative h/c or other parts, but in the end, it is the trend that matters.

An average ratio should be around 110, although it differs from one sector to another. I would still say 110 is an average that any company should reach. My experience shows me the following:

- < 50: very inefficient HR. Probably there is no system in place. Closed to change. Not process driven. Reactive and very high cost to serve.
- 51 to 75: improving efficiency but still needs to focus on the system and also more focus on manager involvement in the HR process.

- 76 to 100: Although it looks like a big range, considering sectorial differences, this level of efficiency tells us that there is an E2E HR system in place. Managers use the system to be involved in the process, to be open to change, and to be more innovative.
- 101 to 120: productive and innovative HR department. HR has mostly automated operational processes, managers are deeply involved in HR matters, and HR has become a strategic and tactical partner to the system.
- 121 >: too much focus on efficiency. Even with a very good E2E system, HR would not have enough sources to function on the strategic part, so it would sacrifice from its services to remain efficient at this level.

I believe the best level to achieve satisfactory internal customer service is around 110. Ratios below that value still require improvement, and values above that put the company at risk of losing focus on the customer. A company would never go from low level of ratio to a higher level by merely by implementing an E2E system. It is a journey and a change program not only for HR but also for the company management style. Therefore, the system is not the target; it is the enabler of the new journey to establish a better service culture with efficiency.

The human resources budget is another important issue. If it isn't made properly, it certainly affects internal customer satisfaction. It is very important for human resources managers to be able to read financial plans. Without reading these, making a budget based on a percentage increase reflecting the previous years' expenses only means allocating more or less budget than needed. Will the business extend? Will there be more sales or growth in production? These questions should be answered. After these are provided by the business unit, the answers to the budget's main questions should be found by collecting important data, such as What will they give us? Do we have a recruitment policy? Do we have a dismissal policy? Will we keep the team as it is? If we go in further detail, the job changes should also be questioned.

For example, company may decide to create manufacturing hubs and also increasing direct sales force instead of sales via distributors. When HR realizes find these facts, it will be more effective budget planning on whom to hire and when, as well as what kind of salary and vested benefits company will give. If the calculated budget is more than the target budget of the company, human resources needs to perform the same activities at less cost. For example training programs would be shifted to hybrid system (a program includes limited class room training but more on-line and self study) from traditional class room trainings since logistic costs would be high and it also would increase cost to serve. Instead in hybrid system, employee can take small part of the training in class and the other part can be studied by oneself, for example, by e-learning. We need to determine budget with the given targets first, from bottom to top, by finding ways of restructuring according to targeted cost level.

9

Reactive HR

Reactive HR follows what has happened; proactive HR shapes the future of the company.

Companies that function without a strategic and tactical plan can only be reactive to the market and to the changing environment. It is common to have a financial strategy for three to five years, but a strategic plan should not only be a financial design. It should have a business, source, and conditional plan through which company directs each management member and employee. Otherwise, we would call it "long-term financial plan." Companies should have strategies that drive HR so that the future can be assured. If you do not have this approach, then, as a consequence, the direction of the company cannot be the desired one, and each unit or department will create its own path to get what they would like to achieve. This will make the company vulnerable to changes that the company is supposed to face. The company starts to follow the market and others to survive. It starts to lose its reason of existence.

As all others, HR also becomes reactive. The company will miss the position of a major department, and HR will only deliver what it is asked for. The main duties or activities become more of a daily duty. There are many examples, but here are some obvious cases: candidates are being interviewed or even agree on compensation details and HR learns about it later on. HR is called to fire an employee on behalf of a line manager or HR would know about a development activity after it took place. In some companies, when there is a change in the organization, the relevant unit and the general manager agree on the terms and changes, excluding HR. HR is involved later in just executing the change. In such cases, the necessity for human resources goes no further than data recording. HR is not a part of the strategic committees or asked to give opinions about any changes to the business plan.

In past years I have worked for both kind of companies, strategic and not. One of the companies I worked for was a family-owned company. Although it was a big one, the decisions were taken by the owner, and major investments were planned only with his blessing. When the planned actions touched the areas that he would prefer to keep as they were, those were interrupted or put aside without being implemented. There were managers who had very close ties with the boss. They acted as informal approval bodies and used to block HR's plans by influencing the boss negatively through the "gossip mechanism," since they were happy with the company's condition at that time, which suited their own needs. Human resources (although I would rather call it personnel department in this case) was inert and reactive as a result of this management style. The company did not survive and lost its power, business, and sister companies. I don't know what happened to those managers, but the boss lost most of what he had.

A reactive human resources merely follows, whereas a proactive one has the power to make strategic and tactical plans in many areas. Human resources determines a vision that is in line with the one set forth by the company and establishes a strategy for major activities, such as compensation, career, development, and succession planning to partner with the business strategy and plans of the company. Work plans focus not only on the current status but also on upcoming years. Developing an appropriate tactical plan with company strategy is a very important process; in this way, HR starts to control and manage the future of the company.

So far we have said that if there is no company strategy, human resources is condemned to be reactive. This is true, but I have also seen cases where the head of HR influences the management and the system of managing HR is very proactive and strong. I would say it can always be a provocateur, changing the minds of managers and ultimately the company. It is not an easy job. It requires experience in management, finance, human resources, project management, and other managerial competencies. In this situation, the head of HR has to push the system to have good relations with top management and involve himself in major committees and meetings as much as possible. This is the only way he can turn actions into strategies and act as a strategic enabler of the company. The most important skill that is required will be speaking in <u>business</u> language. The head of HR should start thinking like the owner of the company, or like a general manager, and foresee needs before they are mentioned. He should be active in meetings to give direction to others, and he should say no to plans that harm the future of the company. If the head of human resources is not strong enough to create his own proactive management style, then in non-strategic companies, management rarely hears about the things he has to say. It does not mean much if you tell your boss that you will do a training or increase <u>salaries,</u> because the company is lagging behind the market.

Therefore, the head needs to learn to read financial data, balance sheet, and profit-loss statements almost at the same level as a financial person and also to be aware of what is going on in the market or in business side of the company. For example, if the company is in the business of sales, the head of human resources should be able to answer questions such as "How much we have sold this month? What is the product portfolio of the company? What do we produce and how do we produce it? What are the market plans?" By speaking their language she can offer HR ideas that will help business managers make better sales and do better marketing. This way, she will have a place at the table of management. Then they will listen more so that HR starts to act proactively. Otherwise, in companies where strategy, budget, and planning are detached, it is not possible to speak of a manager who says, "I do my own way for HR." I would even say that HR becomes a slavery of management to survive.

If company is in reactive mode, HR should watch out another thing. I call this the "Circle of Zeus." This is when the general manager and three or four managers around him create a shadow management circle to manage the company. In this circle, there is only one rule—to serve Zeus. It becomes more important to satisfy the GM than to do the right thing. Does this sound familiar? In such an environment, if HR is out of the circle, it becomes almost impossible to act proactively.

An experience of mind provides a good example of that situation.

I started to work as the human resources manager of a company, and I notice that the company didn't have any human resources policy. It was running with daily rules, and only the financial business budget was planned. Actually, there was not even a department for human resources, only payroll and personnel affairs—that's all. So I needed to create a plan to make HR re-exist in the system and also to change the company culture.

I first decided to listen to other managers and had face-to-face meetings for thirty to sixty minutes with department managers who reported directly to the general manager. I wanted to know about their expectations from human resources, so I asked them two questions at the meetings:

1. What did they expect from me?
2. Was there anyone to replace them in the future?

The first question was answered in an enthusiastic manner. They listened and also bombarded me with the list of the things they would like to receive from the HR function. They also provided information about their communication with each other and many things related to their management style. The second question was a bit provocative for them to answer. Some told me that I cannot ask that question; only a GM could. Some asked me why I was asking. Their replies gave me an understanding of what I was going to face during my journey, who was leading the others, etc.

I next decided to hold a meeting with all managers and present their requests. Mentioning that I had spoken with them, I listed their expectations. I asked their approval to proceed. Actually, these processes were not different from the answers to the questions "What is the expectation of the customer from me? What can I sell?"

In short, our planned activities turned into an expectation list for the managers. We reached the point where we established, "We ask and you deliver."

Of course, while doing this, the human resources manager should understand and find out who is in the circle and test the list to be presented with them before the actual meeting takes place. This approach will ease your path to getting approval and acceptance by others.

In the end, human resources became an important function in the company, receiving the support of the circle, and the circle started to be replaced by rules and governance.

I would say this is the best way to start change in such companies. If the human resources manager had said, "There is no strategy, no target, and no plan, so we need to change" and submit to the GM the plan first, she would not survive with that company for very long. The human resources manager needs to smell out and seek answers to questions such as "How can we plan future better?" and "Who should we work with?"

And, of course, the most important part is to create rules to make company powerful, not to create one's own power. Otherwise, she will crush the wall somewhere, and the system wouldn't work.

Being proactive and shaping the company brings success only if it is achieved together with management. That requires the involvement of all.

Finally, human resources should involve not only managers but also the employees in the work during the change. To achieve this, you can hold workshops and increase the sense of ownership by asking their opinions; this way, decisions are approved by all levels of the organization.

10

Is Training Mandatory?

Development activities are perceived as "good if it happens" unless they are career based. Only then do employees use development as a base.

Training and development activities in companies are extremely important and definitely necessary to manage correctly. Development activities are managed with a general approach instead of annual and position-based planning by human resources and management. This is because the development plan, which is a result of a performance and feedback process based on development, is not prepared effectively enough. If human resources manages development activities according to the internal client's desires, the presentations of development vendors, or the requests of top management, trainings and development activities will unavoidably become populist activities. There should be a balance.

Companies spend between 0.5 and 1 percent of total payroll costs—and in most cases even less—on such activities. Whether this is an investment of the company or an expenditure of operations depends on how we structure the activities. If these activities are not well planned and defined, it is line manager's intention to use them as motivational activities. The general manager or the top manager prefers to use the "corridor management" style, without even informing human resources in advance. In this way, the activity becomes a moment of relaxation for the employee.

Development activities are an important investment of the company. They need as much attention as we pay to machinery or I/T investments.

Anything we plan should create value for four main stakeholders—the employee, company, and system (meaning the culture of the company). I differentiate employee from the person, since they need to be developed separately to have a complete activity. Employee development should be related to the job that person performs; on the other hand, personal development should be based on the individual life of the person to increase engagement and intelligence. Development activity should also create value for the company, meaning that any activity HR plans should lead to better employee performance. Finally, the culture and values of the system should also benefit from the activity. I mention this separately to call attention to HR in this respect. This part usually gets low attention when training is designed. On the contrary, we need to use the time to remind stakeholders of the values and strategies of the company and enforce the culture.

The design phase is important. The questions human resources should ask are as follows:

- Why is this activity necessary?
- What is the real need?
- Is there anything else we need to do before design phase starts?

Long story short, it should approach the issue as a consultant and measure the correctness of the request. Because when human resources start to behave like a consultant, it also starts to educate its internal client. Outdoor activities in particular surprise me a lot. HR should question if there is a problem in a department, if there is a relationship problem between the manager and the employees in a department, or if the employees are not so enthusiastic. Without asking these questions, HR decides to go for the proposed activity, and an outdoor activity immediately happens, in the that all in the department will create a great bond! Monday there will be a new department and a new understanding. Human resources did the job, and the department is happy—problem solved. I wish it were that simple. But this is impossible (at least impossible with the knowledge we have today). Managerial and leadership problems can't be solved with outdoor or activities or trainings.

To do so, it is necessary to build strong systems with strong infrastructures. Why would the employees like to develop themselves? Why do they need this? Believe me, most employees are aware that it is not a motivation activity, but knowing that a training, approved by his manager means they will be noticed, they believe it will somehow affect their careers, so they attend, even if they don't want to.

The solution is to create an infrastructure that allows people to understand the reason behind the training, by linking the development activities to career development so that training and practice happen simultaneously. The employee must know that it will be hard to advance without being successful in this training or development activity. This will push the employee to take the development activities more seriously, and human resources will only carry out the success of the program and career plans together. Surely, costs will be kept under control and effectiveness will be improved. Unnecessary activities will be eliminated, or their number will be reduced.

Only in this way will employee and company get together. Ensuring this will strengthen human resources, and the action will be most beneficial and correct for the company. At the end, it should be harder to get a promotion without fulfilling certain training and development activities, and the definition of these activities differs individually for each position. This is not an easy process, but it is a milestone of a successful system. Instead of preparing a good training catalogue, create a development map extracted from the requirements of the job, depending on the position. Especially in the small businesses, the results and the succession plans can even be followed up manually. Unless you do this, career and learning curve will bring the employee unsuccessful results, caused by premature promotion and a position that is higher than her experience.

As mentioned before, this happens to talents in particular due to their desire to move up fast. I faced cases in which we were pushed to move some talents more than twice in two years. What happened in the end? They left because they did not know what to do with the job, and subordinates killed them because of their lack of job knowledge. They were well trained and developed, but gaining experience and practicing knowledge is essential to keep one's position. The table below is just a simulation of the problem any employee may have in case of an early move or a development plan not integrated with one's career. He can't reach the expected level of performance until the curves are aligned. The gap between these learnings and his career is going to be the pressure zone for the incumbent. The employee will try to fill this gap by focusing on the things he knows and forcing others to follow what he knows. This is going to push the performance level down for the individual and also for the department or unit, if the person is a manager.

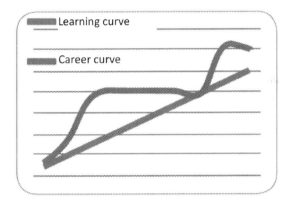

In short, due to this an employee may lose her job if she is an employee at a lower level position; or she can experience unsatisfactory results if she is at higher levels. Big gaps between the two lines, as seen in the graph above, usually manifest as *bad performance, dissatisfaction, shortsightedness,* and *closing oneself to improvement.*

Although there is no ideal curve, in first steps, having a learning curve above your career provides you with a chance to balance your knowledge with your career, and you will be able to keep the performance level sustainable, since you will have a strong learning background.

When talking about career moves, the perception is mostly of an upward one. In reality, a career move can also be lateral to educate the employee for future upward moves. That is why I strongly believe in integrating development plans with the posts of the functions rather than segmentation of employees. I am not suggesting talents should not be given extra development activities, but these should be balanced with the job they are performing so that the learning curve and career curve merge, as shown in the table below.

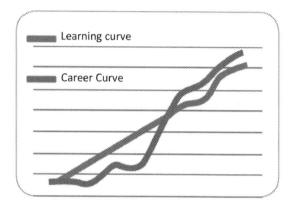

The learning curve should be ahead of the career curve to make sure that the employee is well equipped to perform the job. This is also a vital step for the future sustainable growth of the person and the organization. Development activities should teach how to perform the current job but also provide awareness for the other functions and lines. This way it will be easier to make cross- and lateral moves. In other words, the company will extend the pool of people for a certain post.

11

Proactive HR

An HR specialist should know how to a manage balance sheet, profit and loss, and business values. Specialists who do not use business language will be lost in transition.

Human resources is defined as "supporting unit" in most companies. There is nothing wrong with being a supporting unit or department, but the idea that HR people and the HR manager should stay back and support other departments is not understandable to me. Supporting a project, a function, or a job automatically puts you out of the strategic picture. People will apply to HR only when they need to. Decisions will be taken at some other meetings to give orders to HR to perform. I am sure you have heard things like, "This is a decision we have taken, so we await you to support it." If you say, "But there are some items that we should not be doing," the reply will most likely be, "This is the decision we have already taken, so we expect your full support." In other words, management is saying, "Look, you have to do what we tell you." Guess who will be blamed in case it is does not work.

Human resources should define its position again to have a strategic role alongside management. This means not only being a part of management boards but also being involved in the decision-making process. Here's how to achieve that:

1. Human resources must know how to speak business language. When you go to a manager and speak to her about the reason why

an employee should be developed, that employee's performance should be measured effectively Instead of language that will be understood by management, you are actually speaking in human resources language.

HR needs to know business data and requirements, not at a basic level but at a level that enables it to create ideas for future implementations or process changes. Surely, it is necessary to know the balance sheet as well as the profit and loss data of the company to translate HR language into business language. To be a strategic partner, this is must! If the HR manager says, "It is not my business," we lose the game before we start. Only in this way can HR start to understand if a project is a cost or an investment. We need to know where the expenses are, what the balance sheet is about, and what the sources are.

2. Human resources should always link activities to performance improvement to create value for the business. For example, is providing an MBA program for an employee a good policy or not? Let me tell you, it is most likely a cost that will create no value. This is because it is a development tool, which is a direct investment in the person, and it doesn't provide a significant advantage to the company for the engagement of the person. Nor does it increase the performance level. As a result of the MBA, the person becomes knowledgeable and better educated, but if she doesn't reflect this information in her job, providing this benefit is pointless. Instead of an MBA, it may be better to send her to more expensive training that will provide an advantage in terms of job performance and influence results.

In one company I worked for, we had a policy stating that degree-related educational requests would not be met, even if the leave taken was unpaid. We believed these activities did not add any value to the company, since it ran against our main policy of win/win. We offered MBA programs with associated universities as side programs and covered most expenses in the case of an occupational match. One of the business leaders insisted on sending one of the talents to an MBA program with unpaid leave. As HR, we reminded him of the policy, but he really wanted our approval.

After several discussions with him and the CEO, we approved the unpaid period and also covered a part of his expenses, hoping that he would return. He resigned and sent a letter one year later from abroad.

This might be an extreme example, but at the end, the benefit for the company was nothing, and on top of that, we lost a talent.

3. Managing costs is the most important aspect of HR, now and in the future. If human resources "controls" costs but does not manage them, the company will probably enter a cycle of laying off in bad times and hiring in good times. To manage costs better, the best system I suggest is the grading system, which allows the company to control organizational growth, eliminates unnecessary promotions, brings fairness to the system, and focuses on sustainability. Grading or banding systems are used worldwide in many companies. However, how we use them makes all the difference. I am not talking about a grading system that only regulates the employee level in the organization; rather, I am referring to a system that differentiates job grade from employee grade.

Purpose	Employee grade	Orga grade
Organizational growth	Employees are assigned to the jobs that they can perform at their best	System controls the sustainability and growth of the organization
Span of control	Responsibility and management of subordinates are designed in a way that provides best management of the unit or department and company	Provides the best possible design to regulate the managerial capability of the system

Cost management	Avoids unnecessary promotions or appointments to protect employee and create a sustainable work environment for them	Costs are managed proactively so that the company creates a continuous efficiency culture
HR management	The employee is paid according to the compensation and benefits level attached to the grade. Expectations from the employee is known by management	All mandatory development activities are attached to job design and also compensation; benefit structure is benchmarked against the market

As shown in the table, organizational grade and employee grade do not serve the same purpose. If the company chooses to use employee grading only, then organizational growth will not be managed well, and an unnecessary burden will be placed on the system. It is normal for people of the same grade to report to each other. In reality, this is totally against the organizational grading system since, it does not check job scope or span of control. For example, you can have a manager at X grade and also a subordinate reporting to the manager at same level. This is definitely going to create organizational issues in the future, since the job design is not healthy.

Especially in big companies, a human resources grading system is a must to manage the organization with an efficient and effective structure. On the contrary, in companies that are running title systems, it is common to encounter personnel accumulation in the upper levels, and when the company passes through a difficult time, redefinition of these structures becomes obligatory. When you have an inflated number of managers or directors, you have to reconsider their employment or level in the organization. This is the worst situation a company with human resources has to deal with. Organizations managed with the grading system go through such issues very rarely, as they control recruitment flow.

In our changing world, cross-functional knowledge has become the key to success for companies. If you don't know the working method of your collaborator, if you can't speak in the other's language, your client will not be able to understand you, and you will start to speak about completely different facts. Then it becomes harder to understand their needs. Human resources should read and understand financials and have enough knowledge on business matters to comment as much as business owners. These are the main characteristics that will bring the other perspective to human resources, leading to a proactive management style.

If the company is not institutionalized enough to let HR be proactive, then at becomes a must to give that role to the HR manager. This means the HR manager should be the one who sets the rules of the game for proactive HR management. He has to maintain a close relationship with the other departments, stand by them, and understand the needs of the business. Due to the unindustrialized environment, this is not easy. So how can it be done?

The manager can organize meetings with the business side and listen to their problems in these meetings. He shouldn't just listen to these problems as the human resources manager, but he should also talk about business matters. For example, he should be able to speak about the current status of sales and ask some questions about them while he is speaking with the sales manager. Is business turnover being increased? Could reducing sales be a managerial problem? What is the target achievement for the year? The proactive human resources manager looks for answers to the questions above and wants to reach out and find the real reasons of the problem by detailed analysis. Taking a more appropriate approach, he questions whether the sales techniques, assigned people, or the attitude is correct. This way a plan on expected HR actions can be produced. This will help HR present future possible actions before they come into reality. It is possible to suggest healthier solutions in light of the systematically collected information.

It is important to make these chats procedural with the help of a "situational report" on HR business line presentations, which also include financials. The structure of the report is also important. Reports that indicate, "Three people left/We recruited five people/We are paying X amount of salary/Our performance notes are as follows ..." do not really indicate much. It is possible to prepare reports in a more structured and illustrative way. For example, "Three people left/this rate has increased compared to last year's/We were facing this kind of problems in past years, but we are not dealing with them anymore/Due to current business trends, we are expecting also a slowdown in the market and therefore turnover of employees in certain areas, so we suggest lowering our speed of hiring." It is necessary to provide a wider perspective. With the help of these kinds of reports, it is also possible to make futuristic analyses.

Human resources can request situational analysis meetings even if the business line doesn't. I recommend holding these meetings at least once a month with related departments. If one doesn't come to you, you should go to them and explain. The introverted HR manager who says, "He is not coming to me, so I'll let it go" is destined to see HR in his organization become a support department.

12

4W1H

HR must explain well its actions based on the 4W1H principle ("what," "when," "where,"" why," and "how"). This is because the employee looks to the practice from his point of view, criticizes if it does not please him, and resists change.

Human resources practices mainly involve things that affect people's hygiene factors (wages, benefits, of other basic needs). HR also carries out practices like improvements and discipline in these areas. When all practices are concerned, especially in highly populated places, it is not possible for HR to aim at pleasing everyone. HR cannot guarantee 100 percent satisfaction, because people, their understandings, and their perceptions are all different.

To illustrate, in case where a new announcement declares that all promotions need to be approved by the general manager, people who get along with the general manager will be happy, whereas someone who cannot get along with the general manager will have different feelings. Likewise, if you announce that all shuttle buses will be using main arterial roads, someone living close to the metro station will think that it does not matter to him or her, but someone who lives in a faraway place will think differently. Therefore, you will find out that it is impossible to please everyone by making something to please everyone.

HR should aim at taking steps that provide for the common welfare of the employer and the employee.

Two months after I started working, while researching salaries and benefits, we found out that the salaries at substaff level were too low. We decided to make an adjustment. We proposed a wage increase on an equal basis for a wide range of employees. By determining our policy as the lowest possible salary rage at this company, we tried to fix the life standard at some point. I thought that salary increases would have a strong effect. Contrary to my expectations, upon the announcement of the circular note and the deposition of salaries, we received no thankfull e-mails but many complaining e-mails from the ones who received a normal increase instead of appreciative ones. It was surprising. Some of the percentages of increase were very high to match the minimum level. Then I was not able to understand. Afterwards, I realized that we had acted against the 4W1H rules. Salary increase is an adjustment that relates to the hygiene factor; although people had reacted positively, they did not find it necessary to appreciate this belated increase. They felt they just received what they should have been given in the first place. On the other hand, those who complained had an adverse effect on the hygiene factor. Well-paid people whose salaries did not increase much were complaining about the substaff wages that increased by a good percentage; they were not focused on the low level of the salaries but only on themselves.

Human resources' target should be taking the right steps that will bring mutual happiness to the employer and the employee. Therefore, you need to put your decisions across people very well. Your efforts will not be effective if you think it is clear enough to yourself but don't take employers' perceptions into consideration. HR should be organizing workshops that include employees while taking common decisions. Let's suppose that you set up a new rule and bring about a change in career paths. As it is highly probable that employees will look from their own perspectives to the career changes, you need to bring people from different levels and fields together and discuss the subject. As HR directors and managers, you should not gather around a table and make decisions on behalf of the employees. You need to incorporate into the system the ideas of the employees that will be affected by the changes. You need to gather both managerial and non-managerial employees and discuss the current system, your plans, and their perceptions. You need to include not only the positive people but also the ones who are likely to resist. It will be easier for HR to make decisions that encompass various ideas by gathering employees from different levels and fields, as much as possible, while organizing these kind of meetings. These colleagues will be setting you in the right direction by opposing you at the workshops. Otherwise, these workshops will turn into a meeting of people that are close to your perspective and will prove unsatisfactory. Of course, it is not possible to implement all these ideas, but at least it will be likely to find out some realistic ideas.

Firstly, as a response to the question **WHAT,** you need to express very well what is being done. Detailed explanations about what the change is are necessary. Second, **WHEN** you should do it is crucial because something should first turn into a necessity. When you implement something that is not required, people do not perceive it as a requirement, and it becomes useless in time. This requirement comes from the employer or the employee, and HR should understand both sides. How can HR understand both sides? HR can make employee satisfaction surveys and organize periodic meetings with managerial and non-managerial people. At management meetings, HR should grasp how things are going and what should be done and turn it into projects. You can make a huge mistake by implementing something earlier than needed. **WHERE** could be counted as a part of what since we define which part of the employee gets effected.

A company I used to work for merged with another company. One of the biggest problems encountered in mergers is the creation of a joint-title name structure. How will managers feel if you title them as supervisors instead of managers and supervisors as heads instead of managers? If you the manager as a director, she may misperceive this change as a promotion. Therefore, we had to build a totally new structure so that people do not refer to their past. To do so, we felt the best option was to detach the personal title from the position and quit using the title completely. This way, we would be avoiding any reference to the past, but it was not an easy duty. Surely, we would get back to the title system eventually, but at that time, using the titles might cause huge problems, and it was hard to foresee the outcome.

The situation was not easy. One of the companies was using "administrator" as job title and "chief/assistant chief" for personal titles that indicated level. Considering all these titles, there seemed to be no new title we could use. The other company had more or less the same job title structure: "administrator." However, personal titles that indicate level are not complete titles. These were ranked as "Specialist 1," "Specialist 2," etc. Employees cared mostly about their personal title, like chief, assistant chief, manager, deputy manager, senior manager, etc., instead of their position title. No matter what we did, there would always be a reference to the past.

We then decided to keep the position titles as they were, or use similar names. In the end, all these titles described the job. As for the personal titles, we gave the numbers used at organizational level. For instance, we entitled the employee as "15" instead of "chief." The personal title was "administrator" and "15." This was perceived as a novelty, and the reference to the past disappeared. It was a very complicated process that needed to be explained through one-on-one meetings. To get back to using job titles, organization should be well-sniffed. Implementing something earlier than needed may have a much stronger effect than you expect, and, most importantly, you cannot take HR practices back. You need to think about a practice very carefully before putting it into use. If you grant a company car and then take it back after four years, the employee will never forget about this during his career, because with these kinds of practices, you touch people's hygiene factors, and in a way you are taking away a benefit. You touch their pocket and they do not forget it. Employees always recall the bad things. When people got used to the numbering system and started to talk with the numbers instead of earlier job titles, we thought that the system was well-established, and we started to name the numbers: Specialist 1, Specialist 2, Manager 1, Manager 2, etc. These were numbers as well, but people started to talk about titles instead of numbers, and ultimately we switched to the final title structure. It was a five-year process. We would have had a much tougher process had we rushed into using the titles first.

Explaining **HOW** you will implement changes is also crucial. Will you explain by visiting the employees in groups, or will you explain via training? It means upon deciding "what" to do. You will have to make a communication plan on "how" to do it if you skip planning. People may misunderstand or not understand at all the things you explain. In these cases, you can hardly obtain the expected results. The step "How" is as important as the step "What." Perception is the cornerstone of a successful project or process.

Finally, you need to explain "**WHY**" you are doing it. This is the pitch of the project. It is the core of your change. Why am I changing your salary/position/etc.? Otherwise, people will perceive the change as they please, and this perception will not match your expectations or targets. There will be problems and water-cooler talks will begin. Your practice will finally come to nothing. In the salary increase anecdote, we acted before explaining our motivation of taking this right step, but we failed. When employees do not understand the process, they may assign a different meaning to it.

As you may notice, the new process or initiative is mainly a communication project. HR's role is embedded in this. If people understand what you are doing and also have right to comment on it, then the implementation is there to stay.

13

Performance Systems

Performance systems do not sort out good employees effectively. HR should set up additional monitoring systems like succession, high potential management, and assessment systems in subsequent projects.

Performance management systems, dating back to Frederick Taylor, can be defined as one's aim at increasing his or her capacity to the highest level to get better results.

Therefore, the performance system is regarded as one of the most important steps in HR practices. The performance system sets the ground for differentiating between employees and for transitioning from a system in which all employees work in the same manner to systems like differentiated salary and differentiated premium payment. This is one of the systems used by many companies.

The precondition for the performance system's smooth operation is a good differentiation between employees, and it should be made firstly by the manager. Today, in many cultures, employees experience problems talking about each other's areas of development and mentioning their weaknesses. At the performance review meetings, usually a poor performance or an unsustainable manager-employee relationship will require the manager to talk about the employee's areas of development. Managers and also employees mostly resist or ignore to talk about the real needs to improve or develop. There are exceptions to this situation for sure, but this is what I have generally observed. Naturally, the performance discussed at these kinds of meetings remains remote to reality. If the necessary infrastructure work about the performance review process is neglected, manager will be focusing on what s/he can remember and this usually is not longer than the last three months. You can recall only that period to talk about and try to give examples.

We can say that, especially in relationship-based management types, performance systems do not work. To make them work in this type of management cultures, companies started to use certain techniques, such as forced distribution or so called encouraged distribution. These techniques helped superficial distribution force to be close to the reality; however, they are still far from identifying the real performance, which is the essential part of the work. Employees can be classified under several categories. Below are the most common ones:

1. Excellent
2. Consistently exceeds expectations
3. Successfully meets expectations
4. Do not meet expectations

These categories can be detailed, but it would be better to keep them as plain as possible. The percentage distribution of the employees grouped under these categories in a company can vary with regard to the company's success, as seen below:

1. Excellent: 10 percent
2. Consistently exceeds expectation: 30 percent
3. Successfully meets expectations: 50 percent
4. Do not meet expectations: 10 percent

Companies may use techniques such as encouraged distribution to get these results. Also, they may assign tasks to the managers. For instance, the percentage of excellent employee should not exceed 15 percent within the team; if it does, then this should be discussed in private between the manager and HR; thus, they make a meeting to come to a mutual understanding.

It is not easy to manage this distribution within the company. Managers will generally tell the employee that he or she was asked to provide that distribution with these percentages; otherwise, the employee is a much-esteemed one. The reason is that the manager is reluctant to give the bad points he or she has to give.

We can see here that the most important thing is to build this distribution on a concrete basis. Otherwise, measurement systems based on a competence or value system would not work. As I previously mentioned, the reason behind it is the fact that people refrain from criticizing each other. A further task to perform is tracking the performance system within a target system and getting reliable feedback.

To set up a target system at the beginning of the year, employees should be provided with a target card in which the targets include the details expressed by the acronym "STAR."

SITUATION
TASK
ACTION
RESULT

Tasks should not be available in the targets. For instance, "preparing document on time" is not a proper target because job content already includes the preparation of these documents. In the case where preparation normally takes a month, a target to shorten this period would be more appropriate. We have to keep in mind that the fix compensation assuming paid at assumed level would be set to meet an employees 100% performance at any given job scope at 100%. What I mean is that the fix is already assumes employee will be able to perform all the tasks listed in the job scope at 100% knowledge and experience. So the target should be representing an "additional value" more than what is described in the the job scope. Lets do an example:

Lets say one of the task of the job is: *preparing all the documentation and also reports of the financial figures*

A wrong target would be: *preparing all the documents and reports on time and reporting back every month*

The action is already in the scope assuming employee will perform it on time with correct results and company already covers this in the fix elements without any need to increase the salary of the employee or paying a bonus

A well set target would be: *improving documentation cycle efficiency we have in accounting reports 5% by creating a new process to have 5 FTE saving by year end*

In this example company asks employee to plan an extraordinary action and improve the job by 5%. Also this target suits with STAR approach as: *improving documentation cycle efficiency (Task) we have in accounting reports (situation) 5% (result) by creating a new process (Action) to have 5 FTE saving by year end(Result)*

Here are the most important points: **the target should force the employee's average capacity**, and **it should be feasible**. If the target goes too far, the employee may stop working on it, thinking it is unfeasible, and this will make the performance system impracticable. Employees may perform better when you set a target, increasing the capacity to around 5–10 percent. The target should offer two things: what does the employee do and how does he do it?

"What" should make up 60–70 percent and "how," which includes competence, skill, value, etc., should make 30–40 percent of the criterion for reaching the target. With this combination, the level of performance and whether it is achieved in accordance with the values and skills can be tracked at the same time. This way, it will be possible to make the distribution between good performance and bad performance more reliable.

Nevertheless, this system alone is not adequate. Therefore, a feedback system should be turned on and work well. Notes should be taken during the year to make sure that these are based on the well-known STAR technique. The manager should take notes for the performance during the year to get ready for the year-end. I suggest taking three notes for positive areas and a maximum of two for areas to be improved.

To illustrate, taking a note like the one below would not mean much:

Last year, he told Suzan that "his presentation was not good."
The correct note should be:
Last March, he intervened in Suzan's presentation while presenting to the general manager by saying that her numbers were not aligned before the GM. Suzan got down and ended up in a bad mood.

This note will make things easier for you at the mid-year interview, or a year later, and it will make for a focused interview. Also, it will strengthen the manager's position in the eyes of the employees. The note is taken using the STAR approach.

Situation: GM presentation
Task: Presenting the results by Suzan
Action: He intervened and remarked
Result: Suzan got frustrated

This approach also determines how a manager would talk to him and also makes it easy to understand from the employee side. The manager should also give the corrective action to close the understanding of the employee.

In addition, the company's succession system should be set up; how employees would promote and to which position they will promote should be tested within the system. Following this process, employees should be trained and develop in a planned way to get them ready for the future positions. In summary, we need to consider the process listed below in order to gauge an employee.

1. Performance: By setting a target, we see what and how the employee did.
2. Potential measurement: This can be made by setting up an assessment center or by determining criteria. It should also be backed by some other criteria.
3. Succession planning: You can designate who will be replaced by whom in the short/medium/long term.
4. Training planning: You can include these employees in the respective training programs.

Then, you should test whether employees transform their potential into performance. This is a long-term process. The point to take into account is to determine the employees who do not transform potential into performance.

Employees with good performance should be in for a better future with the company. This is because the underperformers' existence in the company puts too much stress on the employees who show good performance. If I am an underperformer, the good employee will start taking over my tasks. As per the experiences I have had so far, the underperformers usually get on well with their managers and remain in the company by taking their side. To be able to sort these employees, as generally advised, we need to question the employee in many aspects, such as performance, performance measurement, improvement performance, succession, and potential management.

Whenever you come across someone saying, "This colleague is very good. I do not understand her performance assessment result," then you are on the right track as an HR manager. This is because managers generally talk about relationships while proclaiming an employee's goodness. They pay attention to the relationship the employees create instead of their work performance. Looking at it from a more corporate point of view, the four systems I previously put forward should be used.

There is one another important point. If an employee considered as high potential has not been promoted in three or four years, this means he has not been caught by the "radar" and does not have a good "network." He does not have good relationships. When people come to me to discuss career problems, I suggest networking. If the employee is good, then upon networking, the perception will change. HR should keep using these kinds of systems to help employees. To be defined as an employee with high potential or good performance by the manager is not enough. HR should question the perception of other managers about this employee and try to understand their ideas on behalf of the concerned manager. Thus, you should transform the list of high potential employees from the department list to the list of your company by calibrating the employees together with managers.

14

Infrastructure

HR is more concerned with building up process and event management than establishing infrastructure. If you do not build up the HR system's infrastructure and make it a part of the organization, results will depend on the responsible person.

Unfortunately, the absence of infrastructure is a problem we encounter even in big companies. Companies are mainly managed through managers, as they do not have any systemic infrastructure development. Thus, HR's effect is far from being corporate and is getting personal. Under the pressure of this situation, HR can hardly show good performance and actively direct the company. Therefore, there should be other systems, such as performance, succession, hiring, and manning that develop according to an infrastructure supporting these systems in the company (I am not talking about the basic and legally mandatory systems, like payroll). Among these, subjects like annual leave, overtime, and tracking of working conditions are naturally privileged, as they have an economic push on the company.

Apart from these, the infrastructure of systems like performance, career systems that appear to be "not really necessary," should be set up by HR; besides, it is a must to keep these systems for an effective HR. As we discussed, the efficiency of HR served around 100 to 110 percent is possible only with full system integration, which means a single end-to-end system with around 60 to 70 percent of processes managed on the system.

Since managing humans is in any case complicated, HR processes should be simple and understandable to make both the manager's and the employee's life easy. Therefore, the most important point in establishing a system is to set up a very simple process and control it, leaving the decision to the manager but directing him.

System should not decide on behalf of the manager, it should rather direct the decisions taken by the manager in line with the company's policies.

For example in case an employee who does not have the potential, is proposed for promotion, system should be able to reject the proposal but then it should be asking for the manager's opinion and not blocking it. As per manager's reasons and considering it is a valued request of the manager, HR would be making the "system adjustments" where necessary, not only appliying it to that manager.

HR's management power should be backed up by a strong system but must be flexible to change. Otherwise you establish an inflexible system and HR's needs become systematized, or rather the need for HR's decision becomes systematized. At that point, the system may become too inflexible. Especially in big companies, systems may be too inflexible to treat everyone equally. But just like the employees themselves, their needs are also different; that's why it is very important to make these systems flexible to a point and incorporate the manager's ideas.

We have mentioned about two important points:

1. System setup
2. System flexibility

I strongly suggest that before the system setup, processes should be tested through manual usage and what they should look like in their final form should be defined. Then adjustments should be made as per the results, and the system should be fixed. When you set up the system with a definite judgment at the outset, you may be setting up a system that conflicts with the culture and the organizational structure of your company. Accordingly, you may have to make system adjustments over and over again; therefore, it would be wiser to test the system manually first and then, after setting up the main structure, integrate other systems into it.

Setting up these systems may be too costly, but HR has to assure the company that these efforts will result in an efficient work environment. Therefore, there should be a business case supporting your investment. HR does not have the luxury of saying that the number of HR team members has to increase to be able to manage these systems.

If you cannot present the business case, then management will not believe this is a good plan. Therefore, while setting up the infrastructure, this should be emphasized. When you set up the infrastructure, you must include the manager's right to speak and act within the system framework, as this is a corporate attitude. You can alter the system if necessary, but certainly no decision should be taken without it.

Otherwise, as previously said, it will be difficult to make your company a corporate entity. In the case that each employee manages on his own, then decisions will be personal, which will deprive HR's function and make it impossible for it to lead the company.

It is important to establish the company's infrastructure and entitle the manager to decision making within company infrastructure's own procedures. At the same time, HR should introduce procedures to the company as an efficient working method.

15

Development is a Must!

The product of the service industry is "human". Bearing this in mind this idea, HR should measure the implementation of training and develop activities by these measurements. This is the only way to success.

All products of non–service sector companies are tangible. For instance, the product of a beverage company can be seen on the shelves, and the product of a white goods company is tangibly displayed.

In these kinds of companies, all HR implementations as well as all systemic processes are gathered around the product to feed it. However, in the service sector, the product is not tangible or formal. Therefore, people will hardly perceive the product. It is hard to highlight the product and put it on a shelf or process it. But when you look at it from a different perspective and see the product as human, there will be no problem.

A note: In order to make it easier to understand, I am naming human as the product to get the focus on the human side. Of course, my intention is not to say that humans are a product. In these sectors, companies usually put the customer first, and they believe their service can be optimized only by offering a better product and understanding customer need. Well, I am saying this is wrong! Let's say this again, in my words.

The employee is the first so that we can understand the customer's need and optimize our products.

I believe in this. I also see managers saying it but not doing it. So, to provoke this mindset and change our thinking about our employees, I call human the product.

Back to our topic. In hotel management, banking, and other service sectors, if you see the product as human, then your perception will be easier, and all activities, planning, and actions around the product will be implemented more efficiently.

Accordingly, as it would be wrong to shelve semi-finished products, sending employees who have not been fully trained into the workplace would also be wrong. That's why employees should be developed before or after they start working.

The important point is to consider the person you are recruiting as a semi-finished product, which can be regarded as the first phase of the process. In order to get a real finished product out of this semi-finished product, you have to first recruit the right person. As the good raw material provision at the right time is the most important thing in production, correspondingly in the service sector, the most important thing is to recruit a good employee at the right time. If not, even intense training or a good training policy will not work.

As the product is being produced, as per a mold in production, if you can't adapt the employee you recruit to the desired corporate culture and service model, no matter how many you produce, the final product may be different from the one you envisaged. Of course, as the main product is human, this will not be easy to discover. Humans do not come from a single mold, but in the light of this point of view, one discovers the importance of intense training and focus on recruitment. Also, the crucial step will be designing and establishing the corporate culture and recruiting as per this culture. In order to achieve this, one should identify who or what will be recruited.

From the company's point of view, this "mold" is the individual **who can comply with the corporate culture, values, activities, and similar rules and regulations**. Hence, determining these and creating a common language upon practice is crucial.

How should one improve the semi-finished recruited product? The way to improve is measurement. As we produce a product according to a mold, and after the product goes to shelves, we work on improving it through tests and customer service. The same system should be used here, by HR.

Employee satisfaction surveys and 360-degree surveys are measurements to better manage the product. There may be people who think that the approach of considering human as a product is not right, but this analogy is easily graspable by the employee and the manager. It makes it easy to understand and compromise. Therefore, we need to understand that she is a recruit to be processed. Then, we need to make this person a finished product with values and improvement activities and provide continued development by testing. Success is unlikely to come if we do not make these measurements.

Finally, HR's primary task is to perceive the product as humans and direct its work in light of this fact. If HR can perceive that the product is human, it will be more successful and will be able to use the factors around it more efficiently.

A training system should be put into practice and processed with this approach and point of view. Success is systemic adaptation as a result of this training and an increase in the performance level. Providing uniformity is the cornerstone of the service sector. If the service is the same in the chain hotels you stay in all around the world, despite dissimilarities from one country to the next, the reason is cultural and systemic liaisons and good training. The same reason lies behind receiving the same bank services in every branch in a single country. Training should be measured through a proper performance system in the service sector. Employees should take improvement activities seriously and pay attention to them. The key to achieving this is to link training to career.

16

How Should HR Report?

HR reports should be financial, planned and offer enough guidance to attract management's attention. The subject of the reports should be based on what happened, what decision was made, and what is expected.

As we have discussed, HR should use business terminology, highlight profit and loss, and prepare reports according to these points. In addition, HR can't only report from its own point of view. HR reports should be understandable in terms of business. To ensure this, the HR manager should know what is requested by her manager. You may report to managers with different styles. Some managers like to see figures, while some are not interested by figures and place more importance on administrative subjects. Accordingly, HR should not prepare uniform reports; reports should be adjusted as per the manager, the general manager, or the person next to her. To do so, HR should create dashboards to serve for different needs and arrange meetings frequently to understand the requests.

HR reports become guiding reports as a result of these meetings via which everyone has a good grasp of the situation. For instance, telling the general manager, "The employees have worked very well this year. Although the results haven't been good, we should give them a bonus to keep their motivation high" would be completely wrong. HR should make a long-term plan by putting emphasis on the business first. The correct wording would be, "The employees do not deserve to receive a bonus this year, because the results were not as expected. But a bonus from your side with a message would be good, as it would transmit your message and at the same time be a future investment." Of course, this argument should be supported with a report. If you give the reason for your proposal, getting a response will be easier. You absolutely need to have the finance department's help while preparing these kinds of reports.

Besides, in order to get over it, one should work more for infrastructure and arrange periodic meetings by controlling the financials. Also, it is crucial to provide regular and planned reporting. Reporting should be made periodically, and it should not be made with different intervals. Employees should know about the publishing time of the reports and when to expect the next one. HR should be given the right to make inquiries to the managers. When you provide these three basic features— guiding, regular reports, and meaningful data—you take crucial steps towards being a proactive HR. When this is achieved, HR is able to make other departments accept its own practices as a contributor. HR will transform itself from a support department to a contributing one, and this is very important, because if it does not, HR will never be accepted as a counterpart.

Transparency is typically a dilemma, since the data is confidential. However, it should at least be open to HR employees, and it should be periodic. In most cases, people attend meetings to get data and understand what is going on. Therefore, employees spend most of their working time in meetings, and this process becomes unhealthy. It is very important to determine the level of the employees who will be attending the meeting. Adjusting intervals will also make the process healthier. I suggest holding monthly or weekly meetings with HR employees and business unit. The level of the attendees, the meeting agenda, and the meeting notes should be recorded, if needed, and these should be used at the next meeting. In addition to these meetings, a weekly meeting should be held with the project team, and updates about the project should be discussed. Plus, every two months, a meeting should be arranged with the directors and managers to provide an update.

These meetings should not last too long. One-hour meetings with other departments is appropriate. If discussions taking an hour are not productive, this means something needs to be changed. Considering the project updates, presentations, identification of actions, and closure, one hour should be enough.

Getting back to the issue of reporting, HR should prepare reports not only for top management but also for employees. Reports should be prepared on the basis of the "what/when/why" principles. The agenda of the reports we prepare for top management and the employees are similar, but the actions to be taken differ. For instance, when preparing a report on any item to top management, prior to the meeting, HR should discuss the results with each dependant, make an action plan, and then present it. Reports that have not been presented to top management without prior mutual agreement, or ones that are unknown to dependants, generally run into difficulties at top-level meetings, and presentations become unsuccessful.

17

HR Needs Sacrifice

If management doesn't care a lot about HR, work as if it does. One day, this attitude will bring HR to an important level in management's eyes.

Human resources departments of non-institutional companies cannot save themselves from being treated as a secondary and unimportant department. They will exist somehow as a result of a legal obligations, or a result of a "we also have one" attitude. In such companies, the human resources department generally reports to finance, to the administrative coordinator, or even to the legal department. The message is "I, as the top management, don't want to deal with these topics. So you deal with them." This is because management either lacks the appetite for or does not see the necessity of having human resources management speak to business units. In this way, human resources must work at staying away from the administration, and as a result of this, the common issues to be discussed become limited to recruitments and exits, payments, administrative affairs, salaries, premiums, etc. This makes human resources completely isolated and relegates it to the lowest level.

On the other hand, some companies who took steps to become corporate institution understood the value of humans and placed the human resources department at a higher level, as a part of management, to ensure human development. This is a good start and a good environment for HR. The success or failure of HR in such an environment is completely related to the quality of the HR manager. If the general manager or the related manager feels himself close to the HR manager and supports his practices by believing her, she may take the institution to a higher place. However, if the GM feels that the HR manager is weak, then by avoiding paying attention to practices, he can start to impose his ideas onto the system. Unless a balanced approach is taken, this will result in unhealthy results.

For the sakes of the discussion I only focus on the companies where in general:

- HR departments that are not on the strong managerial level or,
- HR departments that are on the strong managerial level but do not receive the necessary guidance and attention

The human resources department, being a contributor, needs to work according to the necessities of the business unit and the company plans. If it does not receive the required guidance and support from the general manager or related upper management, it will lose its motivation and its practices will become routine. It will not exceed expectations but do only as much as required. Apart from being an unhealthy situation for the company, its consequences could be the loss of job satisfaction for the employees and lack of practice and loss of creativity of HR in the long term.

An HR manager should think in this way in order to overcome this situation: Who am I working for and what for?

If your answer is "the general manager" and "for position," you can continue what you are doing and achieve these. Then, with the first general manager change, what you were doing will be changed.

If your answer is institution and employees, then what we are talking about is gaining importance. Human resources, who work for the institution, manage systems and processes in the way they know it is correct. Of course, the key here is to balance the protection of the interests of employee with that of the employer. While ensuring that, the HR department manager protects the interests of the company by using the data and events he has.

For example, for promotion request comes from the managers, but HR thinks it is not correct. HR proves its determinations not with words but with the data it has created by demonstrating and stating. Such as showing that the proposed employee is not in the backup plan. His performance is low, his position in the performance chart is at a low level, or information received about him is in this direction, etc. If your system is strong, this assignment would be wrong and you will be right in long term. When you prove that you were right, the number of managers who will believe in you increases and slowly reaches the position where it needs to be.

This is not something easy. It requires sacrifice, belief, and knowledge. To provide that, human resources must work as a researcher, adopt a questioning mentality, and be a follower and measurer of results. HR must be aware of the importance of what the internal customer and managers say as well as what the rule says. Of course, managers like to do what they want in the way that they know. There are exceptions to this, but this is what is usually encountered. The HR manager must always be in the "A" class. Your position can only be strengthened in this way. The general manager or other managers must respect your practices and ideas. Employees must support you and respect the applications. An HR manager and department who always does whatever management says will not be considered positive by the employees.

Managements are temporary. Also, HR managements are temporary, but strong systems are permanent. At least they are not easy to get rid of.

18

Follow Up

Periodic meeting notes should include information about who is responsible for what and when. The starting point should always be the previous meeting's notes. Follow up is important!

We touched this point in an earlier section. Let us elaborate now to stress its importance. All companies have the responsibility to hold meetings. Meeting notes are a keystone of a corporate company. They provide a corporate memory and prevent the need for personal dependence. Of course, meetings should be held by all companies, but the degree to which they are fruitful and productive depends.

Meeting culture brings to light the working style of the company and even has crucial value for clarifying the company culture. If you are working in a structured company, the meeting starts at a definite time, but if you are working in an unstructured company, the meeting starts upon the employer's arrival. As we are mostly close to unstructured, meetings start when the senior arrives and last for hours. In many companies nowadays, almost all issues are discussed at the meetings. There are a few reasons for this: the meeting has become a habit, the company has accepted meetings as a way of working, there is centralized decision making, there is too much silo management, there is no environment of trust and limited information transparency. Therefore, the meeting agenda is significant for good meeting management. I would cluster meetings as follows:

Informative meetings: Meetings that gather employees to give information via a presentation or discourse. Generally, employees ask pointless and unproductive questions at these meetings. Sharing a very simple presentation beforehand would make this kind of meeting unnecessary. In other words, just share the information with a very clear mail or memo instead of holding the meeting.

Decision-making meetings: At these kinds of meetings, information should be shared beforehand, participants' opinions should be received, and the meetings should be closed with final opinions on the meeting agenda. Though taking a meeting record might be useful, it is enough (and also crucial) to write down the decision—if necessary, a signed one—since the most important part is to make a decision.

Action meetings: These are mainly intradepartmental, interdepartmental, or project meetings. It is a must to take a meeting record including attendees, absentees who were invited, subjects that were discussed and actions to be taken, responsibilities, and the deadline for the actions. This record should be published within forty-eight hours of the meeting.

Surely, there are motivational or budget meetings covering large groups in the companies. However, these are mainly informative meetings. At this kind of meeting, employees listen and take notes.

The number of attendees is normally neglected, but the attendee list should be prepared carefully because the information about the attendees and absentees is important for the other attendees. Especially at decision-making and action meetings, this should be well specified. Accordingly, to determining the list is important because it will clear away the doubts of the rest.

At successive meetings, it is helpful to go over the previous meeting's records. Thus, subjects would receive follow-up and the responsible person to complete its action would make an extra effort. By repeating these actions, they become routine. Especially at decision-making and action meetings, it is crucial to manage the process. Meetings are generally managed by the top-level manager, and in this way the hierarchy at work is kept. During the meeting, actions are discussed by going over the agenda. Any subject that is out of the agenda is discussed at the end of the meeting. However, it is not preferable to discuss the subjects that are out of the agenda when they relate to discipline. The record should be published within forty-eight hours of the meeting. This way, there is enough time for a healthy follow-up.

The meeting manager should be asking questions like, "Do you have any questions?" and "Any comment?" while going over the agenda to create a discussable environment. Otherwise, decision-making meetings will turn into informative meetings.

Because of the increasing utilization of mobile, and smart phones especially, the efficiency of meetings has recently decreased. This is especially true of informative meetings. Since these meetings are more unilateral, attendees do not ask any questions, and they lose their focus. The presenter loses motivation, and the meeting closes with no value creation. For this reason, at action and decision-making meetings, the meeting manager should be able to attract attendees' attention to the meeting. Best way to do this is to ask questions or make comments. It would be good to limit the number of attendees to ten at these kinds of meetings in order to have this opportunity.

Summarize, the way meetings are held is very important, as these activities are an important part of the corporate process. When you analyze companies, you will find out that managements spend three to four hours per day at meetings. As the level rises, hours spent at meetings will increase as well. I think that at least 50 percent of these meetings are pointless. The manager should be asking himself the following question: "Why are we doing this meeting?" "Is it really necessary?" "Can we make a decision without a meeting?" If the answers to these questions are not satisfying, then perhaps the work can be done without a meeting.

If a decision-making or action meeting will be held despite everything, the agenda should be reformed and the attendees should be informed beforehand; responsibilities should be assigned in a meeting record at the end of the meeting. This way, meetings will turn into a control mechanism within the company. This is the format that I have been using in our meetings.

SAMPLE OF MEETING RECORD	
Attendees	Attendees' names to be written
Record	Sender is the person who takes the record
For info	Names of absentees who were invited to be written
Date	Meeting date to be written

Agenda	Agenda of the meeting to be written		
Task	**Status**	**Responsible**	**Date**
Preparation of a line to control production and test.	Preparations have started. Control to be discussed with the engineer of the line.	Production and planning.	April 15
Task to be written.	Latest updates to be written.	Responsible department or person to be written.	Due date

19

HR Should Not Forget It's Job Is Human

The door should be open, and employees should come and talk about their problems. The manager should follow up the solutions. Even if the solution is negative, the process will build trust.

The human resources manager should like to be interested in people; this is the cornerstone of good management. If it's not a part of her personality, then s/he should not do this job. This is the concept that motivates and makes one a leader for this job, as well as for all other jobs. I encounter managers who spend time mostly in their offices, at their desk, working on processes and projects. This kind of introverted manager refrains from making contacts and does not see relationships as a part of their job. However, the human resources manager's essential job is human and not writing or managing processes.

When you start a new job or get a promotion, the first step should be to set up a one-on-one interview with every single employee, from the top to the lowest level. If there is a large HR department, then you may perform this in groups. On these one-to-one, work on the questions beforehand and plan a meeting shorter than thirty minutes. At the meeting, you will see that the employees perceive you as a friendly and at the same time as a good manager. At most of the meetings I have had so far, I have heard employees saying, "This is the first time I have been in this room" or "This is the first time I have talked to someone at your level." A working environment where you are not in contact with the employees, whom you do not know in person, is not a suitable environment for talking about mistakes or tasks. Accordingly, living on your own values in such an environment will probably make you run into a stone wall. To avoid this, you have to pay attention to your working environment.

Firstly, make sure your office is visible. Choose a room with glass walls, and keep your door open. These are the major conditions of being accepted by the employees as one of them so they talk to you about their problems. This will convey the message, "I have nothing to hide," which will combine with the message, "I am ready to listen to the employees," and employees will come to you.

You have let every single employee know that they are free to call or e-mail you whenever they want. I know it sounds like it is hard to manage and a loss of time, but this is one of your most important tasks. Just about all employees have trust issues with their managers. They need someone to look after them, and this relationship should be established with the HR manager or managers within the HR team. Communication channels should always be open. If a problem is disclosed to HR and you follow up and solve it, people will talk about it and the company will score a point.

I want to tell you an anecdote. At one of the company's dealers, in Turkey's Eastern region, an employee had a severe car accident. Though the subject was not directly related to us, we covered all the medical benefits and costs of surgery and helped him recover through therapy lasting more than a year. This was discussed throughout the Eastern region. Surely employees also felt confidence in the company. Human resources should always stand by people but especially by those who need help. This way, employees will take a step towards a sense of belonging, which is at the secondary level, if not the top level, of Maslow's hierarchy of needs. And HR should distance itself from the position of a department that does not properly allocate salaries and side benefits.

Here, of course, the company's approach is crucial as well. If the company's policy is to stand apart from such cases and perceive these as an expense, HR must work harder. However, if it is well communicated, the company is unlikely to be cool towards it. If you still receive a negative response after communicating the situation in detail, then you should bear in mind that you are working for the wrong company.

This does not mean that there will certainly be a solution or a positive outcome when the problem is disclosed to you. Let's say you have been told about a promotion that was not approved and you found out that the promotion in concern was not possible; indeed, this was the right decision. An explanation with details would be satisfactory and build confidence.

Most importantly, the HR manager should see the big picture and question whether a general policy change is required, then discuss it with his manager. This way it will be possible to test whether this claim or issue is a systemic problem.

Employees would like to see the human resources as company's protecting soul, mind, and eye.

Employees would like to feel human resources' support. If they find out that the problems they disclosed to you are not being followed up on and solved, they may no longer seek for HR's help unless it is urgent. Therefore, the management and termination of processes is important. Employees should be informed of this termination. All communications should be written, comprehensible, and confirmed by the employee. Request closing may be indicated by a thank you call or note, a message that says, "Although the result is negative, thanks for getting back." Your message is not enough to solve this issue; the claim's subject should be kept, and by forwarding it to the concerned department, the employee's file or data should be updated.

Another significant point here is to take action upon the complainant employee's approval. In cases where the employee is complaining about her manager or another employee, as this is a delicate matter, it would be better to ask the following question: "This is an important matter. Would it be okay if I presume this discussion to be an official meeting and take action?" Employees sometimes need to be told this to communicate. Things that they disclosed to you may be confidential. On the other hand, if the employee discloses to you something that should be disclosed to her manager, then you should suggest to that employee to communicate it to her manager first. This way, there will be an opportunity to solve this issue within the corporate hierarchy. If HR tells the employee, "Okay, I will forward it to my manager" or "I will handle this matter," then by damaging the employee-manager relationship, you might make things worse. To sum up:

- It is hard for someone who does not love human beings or being close to human beings to work in a human resources department. It may be harmful for both this person and for the employees. The human resources manager should be humble. The HR manager is not the company's guard; he is rather the one who takes the necessary measures to maximize the relationship between the company and the employee.

- The HR manager should be transparent and keep the office door open while working, ready to communicate. This is necessary to talk to people and assist them with this relationship.

- When the problems are disclosed to the HR manager, she analyzes them and asks the following questions:

  o Should I solve this problem myself?
  o Is this a claim, or is there any need for a systemic change?
  o Should the employee talk first to his manager?
  o Can I solve this problem?

- The HR manager manages the process and makes sure that the employee understands the result by getting a confirmation, which is documented and kept.

Human Resources is a department that should be close to the employees and especially work to identify and solve the problems between the employee and the manager by talking with both sides.

To ensure better performance, the HR manager should have a different profile. Here are some suggestions. Just to repeat:

1. Transparent office. A closed and walled room where no one enters may be scary to the employees. An environment hiding things going on indoors disturbs employees, and it affects the entrance and the exit. It is distanced. This is an outdated type of management that cannot manage the new generation, because people request being in touch. They need to explain their problems themselves and to be heard even if there is no result. The first

condition for this is a transparent room. This situation conveys the message, "I am in the center, but I am transparent."

2. The HR manager should work within the department, among employees, rather than her office. If the HR manager has free time, she should visit other departments and spend time with employees. In formal dialogues, thoughts are being filtered before being expressed; informal dialogues are more like a friendly conversation. Create an environment where employees feel free to talk about their ideas and things HR would like to know about. If an HR manager is looking for such an environment, she should surely create a friendly conversational atmosphere. Ask employees about their work or family; engage in topics that will create a friendly environment. It's important to create such environments, because, by nature, people forget about the salary increases or other things, but they never forget these small emotional things and are likely to recall them in future. Managers that can affect people emotionally are generally successful people. This kind of transparency is one of the factors that helps people tolerate the system.

Many people cite salary as their reason for resignation; however, the underlying reason is often people's behavior. Therefore, a human resources manager who serves as a model for creating a transparent, supportive environment sends a message to the employee, to the customer, and even to himself. Because a manager working in a transparent environment feels the necessity of being transparent. The loss of this kind of environment and the contact in between will result in culmination of small problems requiring harder solutions.

Humans intrinsically aim at increasing their awareness; we can get a feedback as long as we support them. Especially for the new generation, this has become a must-have. Another important point is to balance the relationship between employees. One should know all employees and spend time with everyone. In this transparent environment, following a social question addressed to an employee and asking the same question to others from time to time is the key to balance in transparency. While creating this social transparent environment, talking about oneself and one's own mistakes is a good step towards relaxing others.

A target-oriented attitude is the addiction of our age. But being indoor rather than being in a transparent environment points another target and gives the following message: "We are different and we can hardly get in touch." It also means, "I delegate to you. If the outcome is negative, you are the responsible. If the outcome is positive, I will get the credit." However, transparency rests on the idea, "We do it together. We share the success and the losses." This means both empowering and conferring responsibilities. In terms of being target oriented or people oriented, human resources has to serve as a model and sustain its position.

If it is hard to find a people-oriented manager, but it is important to choose people who score high regarding transparency and sharing competencies at behavior and personality tests. Self-improvement and skill improvement are possible. I think that it is much more important for a manager to use her heart together with her mind than the name of her school.

20

Layoffs Are Also Branding

Similar to recruitment, layoffs are also "active branding." HR should measure these processes and should make an action plan by analyzing them.

HR mainly (and naturally) pays more attention to recruitment than layoffs. When you make an erroneous recruitment, training, improvement, and career activities will be built on a wrong basis; therefore, it is crucial to choose the correct person for the correct position. There is a good level of effort for this cause at HR, including personality analysis, culture works, and employer branding to find better employees. HR visits universities, makes presentations, and runs contests. The ultimate goal is to bring in the most talented and best employees, but in fact, the most important point of recruitment is what happens after you hire the employee. An employee may feel good when he just starts the job, but after a while he may find out that the situation does not meet his expectations, because in time HR may tell "white lies" for branding and the employee resigns when he notices these in due time. Therefore, your behaviors after recruiting an employee and your level of honesty at recruitment matter as much as recruitment itself. Research shows that the number of resignations at an employee's first year increases if the employing companies create a virtual world by not reflecting the truths in branding.

Another step of branding is your relationship at the employee's resignation. The management of the resigning employee is under not only HR's but also the whole system's responsibility. If it is well managed, the concerned employee will present you as your cultural attaché. If the resignation process ends positively, the employee will offer praise. If it ends negatively, he will denigrate you.

I believe the unemployment or resignation process is as important as recruitment so that the company can have better turnover, management, and branding.

Why the employee leaves us is the basis for why the employee should be choosing us. If the reasons are not supporting each process, then the employer branding diverges from reality. The company should understand the reason of leave scientifically. Of course, the process and reasons of unemployment differ from those of resignation. However, the consequence they create share some resemblance. They both affect the remaining workforce negatively if not managed well.

Resignation:

HR should build warning processes to understand the reasons why the employee resigns and a maximum level of fairness and effectiveness should be exercised during the resignation process. This is important for the employee resigning but also for the peers remaining to see that company is acting in the best possible way to treat its employees well.

HR and management are usually not good at managing resignations; they may think it is unnecessary, as the employee is leaving anyway. Management may push the human resources department for an immediate separation of the employee they do not want to work with, feeling the sentiment of being "left" by the employee. Though the resignation process of an employee who has worked twenty years is technically the same as the one of an employee who worked two years, emotionally, the first may need to be managed differently. As per my experiences, I believe HR should have basic rules of treatment for all, then differentiate the service rules depending on the level of the person. The base rules should consist of definitions, including fairness, transparency, communication, leave day, and payment time. From these basics, HR can differentiate rules per seniority, department, or other clusters. You may offer the individual outplacement (a service offered for the employees who left the company to guide, assist them to find a job) to managers and a group one to employees. Though outplacement is not a common practice, it contributes much by creating value, and as far as resignations are concerned, HR should not consider it as a cost. The more turnover company has, the more important it is to manage the process well.

By applying good policies and being consistent on the process, the company may even lower its turnover rate and lead cultural change for a better workplace.

Another common mistake is to grant salary increases or bonuses to resigning employees, under management pressure, in order to dissuade him from denigrating the company. This is reactive HR management. What needs to be done proactively is to act before an employee resigns, and it is a long-lasting issue that is related to the creation of an environment in line with the employee and the culture. If the employee has gotten to the point where they have been pushed to resignation, my suggestion is not to stop her because, as per my experiences, these employees lower their performance level, increase their expectations on hygiene factors, and may resign later in any case. So the first goal is to act proactively and avoid resignation, and the second is to ensure a well-planned separation in case resignation.

Exit interviews should be performed to create value for the future. Though the employee declares all details to HR at the interviews in the case of resignation, she may still think that nothing will change. Therefore, it is crucial to change these interviews into structural documents, highlighting some important points. HR should convert the information of the resigning employee into messages as follows:

- Management—mentioning the manager style, what is needed to correct, such as coaching, training, etc.
- Process—a message to HR to test whether HR should consider changing the way something is managed.
- Business—let them know if the business side should consider changing something for the better or create a more efficient way of managing the job.

Redundancy

Apart from resignation, there may be employees we do not want to work with. In case the employee opts for resignation, he should fully understand the reasons for this reluctance. This is possible by using performance systems—feedback meetings and warning systems. The employee should leave without queries.

As we discussed, performance systems do not always give the message the employee should hear. If the results are positive, managers either choose to say nothing important or say too many positive things. If the results are negative, managers decide to give a rating higher than deserved to make their life easier. So, at the end, the data HR uses in redundancies are not really accurate. That is why HR should definitely question the manager before taking any action:

- What is the reason we are un-employing him?
- Does your request match with your performance rating? If not, why did you change your rating within the given time?
- Has any feedback been given to the person so far?
- Has any development offered to the person?

This way we can better manage the process. I have encountered situations where the manager did not convince HR, so we did not perform the redundancy. We asked the manager to make the employee understand the situation s/he is in. If it is not clear and also employee put valid arguments on the table than company may give that employee a chance, with more training and coaching to see if the situation is improving, following a good feedback session together with HR.

In any case, HR should state in the policy that if there is no specific reason of redundancy related to a disciplinary act or ethical conflicts, the employee may be transferred to another department. If an employee is not content at her current position, the company should look for other available positions within the company. In case the employee does not have any ethical issues, we can create such an opportunity by evaluating the process through interviews. It is possible for employees to perform astonishingly well at the positions they enjoy. An employee who is transferred from another division is usually expected to be unsuccessful, but we should be patient because performance is likely to rise in time. These kinds of transfers are more easily practiced in small-sized companies. Although it is not entirely possible, it would be efficient to practice the same in large companies as well.

It is, in any case, a very hard process. It has never been easy for me. I think the best way is to convince yourself first, and then the employee, that it is not working. Again, the process should be fair, transparent, and communicated well. This is surely very important for the remaining people. A communication plan should be developed for the remaining people. Another key to success in this painful process is to act fast and accordingly.

21

Competent Jerks

An immoral manager with high performance is the system's virus. Although management defends him, HR should determinedly defend the opposite. That's how trust is built.

In recent years, companies have placed too much emphasis on performance and overemphasized the evaluation of the performance card. Employees with low performance scores are not being appreciated, and it makes employees think that success only comes by reaching targets, expected results. The employer does not much care for the level of stretch they put in the targets, but rather they just want to get results.

I was in the elevator once. Since we were with one of my colleagues in the elevator, I greeted him by asking, "How is it going?" The reply shocked me

"At 90 percent, so I am doing fine."

This response told me that we had created a system in the company that disregards "humans." We were asking them to be machines. This is a very bad feeling for a person. For them, happiness meant reaching their target. They focus everything on performance, whether they are at 90 percent or 92 percent. All they care about is the promotion they will get, and unfortunately, this is what the system requires.

The world is not the same as it was before. Our expectations in life move more to hygiene needs, where only psychical requirements are met. We want to buy a larger TV with a larger house and a big, nice car. Our children are spoiled and ask for anything they want. This is a cycle of death. We want more, and companies work more to serve. There are more companies doing business in different segments, and we want to make more money to buy more. This mindset led to 2008 crisis and I think more to come. We lose our humanity to money.

Back to our topic. In the end, the system creates its own monsters. These employees are successful, but they harass everyone. On the other hand, per the theory, we need to have employees who still reach their targets with manners and respect of the rules and the peers. Aggressive employees create the assumption that they are successful and powerful, but this is shortsighted, as they usually do not create value in the long term. This culture starts to poison the company, as they become successful by oppressing others. Ultimately they occupy senior level positions and hire employees like themselves. As this culture expands, real and prospective managers are lost within the system. As for the concept of management, these people care about others just for their self-interest. As their sole focus is their self-interest, this insincerity disturbs other employees and they do not respect them. Although they are aware, employees do not talk about this situation. There are many examples of this. Some of these high performers face ethical faults, and when this fact is disclosed to top management, the reply comes "Yes that's true, but he is successful." The message is clear that management does not want to terminate them. I have seen employees rewarded for their success in selling the best ever number on a product. The general manager calls them to the stage and gives them a reward. She is given a free holiday to a very nice location. The company is given several culture-killer messages here:

- Employee: Your way is the right way. Kill all others. Do what you can do best.
- Other employees: You are failing because you are not aggressive enough. Do as the winner does. Go and kill.
- System: This is the new normal, so get used to it. We will tolerate the way they achieve and ask you to cooperate.

The company starts bending the ethical code and regulations to let these employees survive in the system. Then days go by and we learn through an audit or other means that the winner actually cheated the system to make those numbers or pushed so much that she created a big number of uncollected receivables. The company cannot even get the money.

This is what the manager starts saying: "I tell you to do this and in return I will give you a nice bonus and also make sure you get promoted," and it even amounts to exploitation. This way of work life leaves no room for social life. People working 24/7, with no work-life balance, are being exploited. They don't realize they are being milked by the system until it is too late.

On the other hand, employees with sense of culture and ethics and an understanding of actual success are the ones who think prospectively and who highlight the company's sustainability. They also have high performance, but on the way to success, they listen to others, give the right to talk, and ensure their participation to management.

The essence of the job is managing and standing by people. In companies that overlook this fact, financial figures do not bring a continuous success. Such companies work by focusing completely on success. Managers have no clue what to do and how to fix problems when they fail. Managers who get overstressed decrease performance. It is vital to take advantage of failure, to lose and to recover. These kinds of companies and employees are unsuccessful at this.

HR should provide an environment in which managers express their feelings and ideas about the named employees. Therefore, as management It will be possible to reach a shared evaluation of the employees. Organizational succession planning meetings provide an opportunity for this. At first, these meetings back up the process, and in time, as these are repeated correctly, people start to shine trough.

Secondly, ethical and disciplinary rules should be well organized and followed up by HR. Ethical and disciplinary rules systems are organizations that discipline and encourage proper behavior. HR's task is to make these kinds of employees transform into better employees by demonstrating both sides' faces to management. HR should "educate" management to make them understand how disruptive their way of business is.

So how can human resources influence management to change this understanding and have a more sustainable approach? That is not that easy. The company under pressure from the board and shareholders to create profit and create it now! Competition is very high, and every company in the sector is trying to get results fast. To overcome this issue, HR should have some basics:

- Accurate data is available to everyone.
- Human resources works with a proactive approach, meaning the department is represented at management board level, business leaders are called to work together on major strategic programs, and HR employees are fully aligned on the needs of the business.
- Management trusts HR and depends on HR to align the system.
- Line managers are open to change.
- Regulation is in place to control the overall sectorial acts.

In addition to the above, human resources should consider employees' development by providing a link between the employee and the strategy. This also affects the way the company manages its business targets and brings bottom-line expectations to a manageable and bearable level.

22

HR as a Coordinator and Consultant

While working with other department managers, HR should led them to take decisions. HR's role should only be as a coordinator and consultant.

As mentioned, human resources should be a contributing department. One of the most important qualities of this role is to provide communication by making sure that its decisions and practices are embraced by the concerned management and managers in its processes. This way, HR would work more freely and for the company in a system-provider role. This is important because HR is essentially performing its task by being involved in other departments' works. The bottom-line most related to human resources activity is employees' cost to the company. The rest mostly involves helping other business or competency functions to achieve their goals. Even when HR manages costs, it very much relies on the actions of the business or competency side. Therefore, HR by nature is a service department, and it should act as a provider or consultant.

This is a fact, but in, reality HR mostly prefers to own the process so that they are perceived as a decision point within the organization. That means when human resources is defeated by its ego, we often state our ambition by saying, "HR did it," "It's our responsibility," or "HR accomplished it," ignoring its reason for being. HR traps itself and starts taking over duties that were supposed to belong to line managers of business and competency. Guess what. Managers like not having to do so much and always blame HR for failures. HR becomes a subcontractor of the jobs that manager does not want to do. In other words, seeing that there is such a function, they even abstain from doing that work. Because, as its name implies, "human" resources is related to people, and managers mainly prefer that human resources take over these kind of works, as it is hard to contact and manage people. This is a very unfavorable allocation of duties. In this case, at good and bad times, human resources may have to undertake management's tasks. In effect, managers generally undertake the good things, and this results in a reactive human resources department.

Human resources become a slave of the management. it starts to have less respect from management and also eventually from the employee side since it mirrors what the management.

In a proactive human resources management style, HR would not say, "I accomplished." The correct statement would be "We helped you to accomplish." HR would be in the middle of employer and employee to create an environment where both sides win for the good of the company. The manager establishes communication through the employee and starts to act as a human resources manager. Human resources may stand by the manager—in fact, it should—but employees should consider the concerned department as the business holder and not as the leading and managing function. This is very important.

We mentioned earlier that managers should think like human resources managers. What I mean is from this point of view, human resources would hold the processes of performance management, the salary system, discipline or merit, and reward, etc., and keep them at an efficient and effective level for the system. Therefore, managers should be accountable for the practice of these processes and its results. HR should prefer to manage these through the managers, and managers should be the main communicators for the results and the situation. The consultant role is to establish the process design, set up the infrastructure, and place department managers at decision points by keeping the human resources managers at the control and backup points. For example, at a new development activity launch, the department manager should talk instead of human resources. Orientation programs should be designed in a way that the manager performs for the employee. Or, let's say you are hiring someone. The human resources system should entitle HR to say, "We met together with you and liked this person at the interviews. Here are the salary levels between quadrant 1 and the median. You can give any salary in between, and these are the salaries of your current employees. Please assign a salary level and then we can talk about it later."

Here, human resources' role is to set the interviews, make a short list of candidates, and then reduce the number of listed candidates to two or three by making interviews together with the manager. After ranging interviews for the last candidates and then asking the manager what the salary will be, the manager will check the system and determine a salary. They will then prepare the contract with this salary and ensure that the manager forwards it to the candidate. Be with manager to help in the process. Therefore, human resources mainly has to manage the process. But the infrastructure should be strong to ensure such management.

Human resources' consulting role should not transform it into a subcontractor. For instance, if the manager says, "I do not have enough time to meet the candidate. You can meet her. Then we will decide on hiring her or not," human resources should not accept it. This is not consulting. In defining the line well, HR should say, "No, it is your job. If you need my help, here are the processes. We should check. Or I will come over and we will talk. But you definitely should do it."

23

HR Should Be amongst People

HR should be amongst people and follow up the informal structure to get results for the benefit of the company and the employees.

Formal organizational structure is the key to any company. This tells us how the company is managed, what the preferred managerial style is, and whether the company is lean, effective, and efficient. It is also major consideration for human resources management. It will be the input for career, performance, compensation, development management design, and cost management.

On the other hand, there is always an informal organization that is usually much more powerful than the formal one. The formal one is where HR puts programs based on the official processes. However, the real decisions are usually taken within the informal organizations. The sample that I put together in the first chart is a typical company chart where we see a GM and three direct reporting lines. Any HR-related topic is discussed within this frame and signed off with the represented official hierarchy. The second one is instead a more complex one to understand. The GM has more close ties with production and the warehouse manager, probably because of their common past or better relation. So each different color shows a different informal relation network that manages the daily life of the company. The informal structure should be discovered to understand how it is valuable for managerial success.

Especially in companies where the corporate culture is not well established, apart from the organization that is shown and drawn, there are informal organizations within the decision mechanism, some of which are stronger than the formal ones. For instance, there is a boss and a general manager reporting to the boss. Let's say there are four deputy general managers under the general manager and directors and managers reporting to the deputy general managers. From the perspective of relationships, the boss may prefer to work directly with the director and take a decision bypassing all other levels. But he would never propose him as the deputy general manager. This is a situation that should be accepted as it is and discovered in terms of management. It is hard to change that situation.

I had a job interview with the general manager of a company I used to work for. The general manager informed me after the interview about the requested starting date. We agreed on a date and I started to work. Then I told the general manager that the official hiring was done but I had to meet all deputy general managers and talk to them one on one to really understand the network management and also to get approval in their minds. While talking to them, I was also trying to test and understand the informal structure through their style and speech. At later meetings, I came to understand that some of them were talking to each other to evaluate me. So when I asked the other one the same questions in the meeting, that deputy general manager started to tell in a detailed manner that a normal reply was supposed to be a short one. So he was actually telling me they were commonly thinking about my question. At the subsequent meetings, the answers started to become completely politicized. In fact, I received no responses that were helpful. Similar conversations we had later on showed that the general manager was not really a general manager. One of the deputy general managers in fact managed the company, because all the others had to get his approval in almost every respect. This meant that this deputy general manager was the head of the informal structure.

It may be nearly impossible to change an informal organization unless the company changes the management. HR should definitely discover the informal structure to be effective from the beginning. Only then can HR bring innovation, corporate culture, and other necessary practices to the company.

For this reason, besides being experienced, HR managers should have high EQ, be humble, and be good listeners. They should not be telling but listening. What do people say? Who looks at whom at the meetings? Who talks first and who talks next? Who comments before the final decision is taken? These are very important.

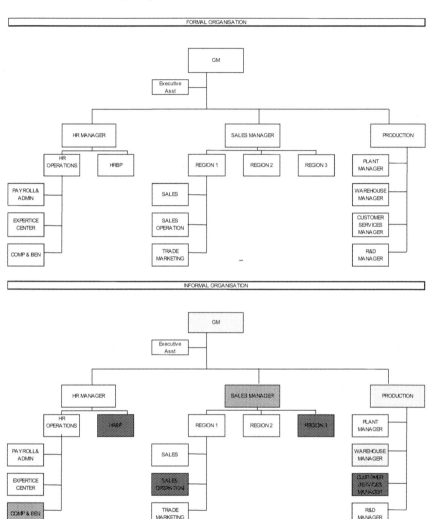

Another important step for a better start is to think like a general manager. This is something I always applied in my past to bring a broader view to my management style. What does this mean?

If I am a manager of a section and reporting to a department manager, my thoughts are usually limited by the scope I have in my job. I do not believe and support this. I think I should be thinking like the department head or even higher to extend my job and increase my ownership. Let me give you an example. Let's say we have four regional sales managers. They each have a different customer base, with different conditions, but almost same budget targets. If each thinks within their region, they would be enemies of the other regions and try to protect their own territory. But if they think like the sales director of the company, then they will help each other, grow together, and create a better environment. This way, the sales manager becomes a sales director in her vision and acts accordingly. Managers become limited by their reality if they cannot think a level or level higher. This is because they get stuck with the management of daily process and focus too much on target achievement rather than success. A manager should take a back seat when needed, focusing on thinking and planning by asking oneself, "If I were the GM, what would I do?"

Human resources should do this more than other line managers because HR is the one driving the organizational facts and cultural changes of the company.

There is no way to resemble the informal and formal structure. Because wherever there are people, personal ambitions, power clashes, and eagerness exist. Even in a family, who is the head of formal and informal structure, Mom or Dad? When you begin a relationship, there is a formal one and an informal one. Some relationships go on for so long that the participants understand each other without even talking. That kind of relationship is hard to break off so the best option would be to manage it.

So as not to overweigh or overlook the individual in the formal structure, human resources should reckon and foresee each move and the reaction it will get in response, just like playing a chess game. This means HR should think ahead of the things that will follow its actions. Let's go back to family example and talk about a tactic that most of us use. Let's say the kid wants to go to the cinema with friends in the evening. Who should the kid ask first for permission, Mom or Dad? If the father is the formal head of the household, the child should ask to the father first. But as the child knows that the mother manages the process and the decisions, she is the one to convince first. Then the kid tells the mother, "Please talk to my father. I want to go the cinema." If she is convinced, then you have the informal leader's support. The mother, as the informal leader, will help the kid go to the cinema in some way. The kid will even have right to ask the father for money. Management is politics. Human resources cannot keep out of it.

HR cannot achieve these if it thinks only mathematically and focuses on the processes. What if it does so? First the kid goes to the father.

"Dad, can I go to the cinema?"

Dad asks, "Have you studied?"

The kid replies, "I will do it tomorrow."

The father concludes, "You should study first."

It is locked! Even the mother option is out now. She cannot be the mediator anymore. This example works if the roles are reversed as well.

Human resources should act strategically while using the opportunities to institutionalize and should know how to get the support of the both formal and the informal structure. Your success depends on the approval of the deputy general manager, the head of informal structure from whom the general manager, as the head of formal structure, gets information. The general manager evaluates the cases with the people around him by asking their opinion about the applications, and she even gathers feedback by asking about the HR manager.

Human resources should always be in touch and connection with people to be able to manage such relationships. It should test the informal structure by making frequent visits. Is there any change? It should ask peoples' opinion and get approval. It should put its practices in place without hurrying so that these become a part of institutionalization and supported by people.

The key here is to use all these for the good of the company and create a better industrialized company over the years. Otherwise, HR becomes a part of the informal structure and fails when the informal fails.

24

You Are Only As Successful As Your Customer

When it comes to people management, the success of the internal customer service level is directly proportionate to the consciousness level of the internal customer.

Employees should be considered as customers in every respect. The general manager, top management, mid-level management, and employees are all customers. If the company's real customers are not the employees, it is almost impossible for the company to give proper service to the external customers. The company should first win over the internal customers. If human resources does not work with this perception and belief, then the company's mentality will be based on the following idea:

We have employees who serve our external customers.

This means that employees are managed with the idea that they are obliged to serve. However, the correct act would be to win the internal customer's mind and heart. Employees should not work in the company but partner with the soul of the company. Otherwise, customer service to external customer will not be sustainable. This is because only satisfied and recognized employees are ready to create positive outcomes.

Outdated thoughts like "Let's cut down on the expenses. There is no reason to spend so much money on training. We are paying them to do the job" are still very common in most companies. It is a challenge for human resources to balance these efforts by standing strong and presenting the case for why it should be otherwise. If management considers that the sales attributes of the market has been changing fast for the last ten years because customer behavior is shifting, it should also consider that the needs of the internal customer are changing and shifting to another level. If this is not the mindset of the company, the company will probably not be able to respond proactively to market changes.

In a constantly changing environment, employees should be equipped to cope with the environment. The old days of hiring more people to do the job are over. Companies should be efficient, effective, and proactive to manage change. The manager is the most important part of this process. The success of the outcome depends on the manager's understanding of people. I am not only referring to people management but also to understanding humans. Someone who understands humans is in a good position to learn how to manage. However, a manager who does not have this skill will not get an effective outcome no matter what system you establish. A manager who knows humans has an appetite for learning the issues related to people and management. This is one of the most important attributes of a manager. If a company has a general manager like this, then HR will have an easier job.

Human resources should establish systems and succession planning to promote managers with this mindset. This should be the first requirement. Then the rest will come.

I was having a succession planning preparation meeting with one of the managers in a where I worked in the past. We were talking about the high potentials and high performers of the department. He defined a high-potential employee with the following phrase: "She is a potential. She could even be a GM in the future because she works with me for long hours, sometimes until morning, to finish the job." The manager was assumed to be one of the high potentials of the company. His understanding of what makes a good employee unfortunately ran afoul of the ethical codes of the company. I tried explained him why she is not a high potential but might be a high performer, since she worked so hard. He needed to consider what kind of value she was creating after all those long hours of work. The manager challenged me and tried to stick to his decision. The same overworked employee left the company, saying she liked the company but could not stand the manager.

The impact of the manager on employee engagement is much higher than any HR policy. HR should help management assign managers who treat employees well to protect HR policies and programs. A good manager will change the perception of company culture and increase the engagement of people despite any problems the company may have. A good manager can convince employees planning to leave the company to stay. In a world of changing and developing relationships, there is no room for managers who do not understand humans. The more a company promotes ignorant managers, the more it will lose its ability to manage change and serve the customer. If human resources management operates in a company where people are secondary and management's sole priorities are sales, profit, and efficiency, it has no chance to manage the internal customer well.

In such a situation, the solution is to establish a centralized HR management according to human resources practices. This way, the system will be educating managers, drawing the line for human management. Centralization should be applied until the company is sure that, despite various personal behaviors, most managers adjust their style in accordance with the stated practices. This might take two to five years of practice.

HR should be the one to continuously set the example, as a department and also as a provider, applying the rules and processes without any change, or changing only the ones that support further alignment of what company should achieve. Practice is the key here. The HR infrastructure should enable managers to practice the system. If this is not the case, then, as we said before, it will be very hard have a common understanding of daily operations.

After this period of adjustment and settlement, HR would switch from centralized to decentralized management by transferring practices to the line manager responsible for the system. This move also is not easy from and HR perspective, since HR willingly give ups the power over processes. If HR thinks proactively and sets its mind as the provider, then this becomes doable. Good internal customer management is the basis on which customer satisfaction is built. Human resources is the focal point for creating that basis. It should help management, but even if this situation makes HR face difficulties before the management, it is to be done for the sake company.

Finally, HR should segregate internal customers as such we would do for external customers. A typical segmentation would be top management, managers, and employees. Then products and channels of service should be defined to better serve the client.

25

Are We Ready?

A project that is applied ahead of time is destined to fail. HR should test all projects in terms of timing to see whether or not the system is ready.

Many applications are evaluated, planned, and executed to achieve a better work environment for the company and its stakeholders. These systems bring an easier way of working and in some cases even innovation to the world of human resources. Practices on performance management, skill management, training, and organization are reconsidered every day to find improvements. Humans are complicated to manage and difficult to understand, and there may be several solution to a single problem. You may choose the one you think is best for the company, but it is not suitable for the employee, or vice versa. That is why we set a culture, with rules and regulations, to control behavior and feelings. We define what happiness is for all parties. In a very hierarchical company, we create an environment where the employee will feel happy if they join a top management meeting, where they have the chance to stand up, ask questions, and get recognition from the manager. We feel proud and touched when we receive a good salary increase and sad when we don't. Human resources plays a vital role in setting the standards and creating the right rules for all parties.

Since humans are complex beings to manage, human resources should launch systems to let HR employees deal with things that matter to both employees and employer. However, bringing new HR practices and systems into use just before change needs to happen will drain initiative. Human resources should not launch things just because they are fashionable or work in other institutions. Human resources should test to see if it is the right time. I call it "smelling to act." It's just like a new product launch. If you launch the product at the wrong time, you cannot sell it, because people will not need it at that time. Accordingly, HR should manage the need. This can be done through surveys and tests. When making a project, HR can share it with employees, measure the reactions through workshops, and test whether they are ready by making visits and talking to them. People usually state their opinion directly and clearly while having one-to-one conversations and consultations. Reading between the lines and having face-to-face discussions will also help you to understand the real need.

Let's take a look at a real incident. In one of the companies I used to work for, I realized that there was no salary and side benefits for management. The salary system was shaped according to the person's or manager's power. My investigations and conversations with directors showed me that company was not culturally prepared for a systemic salary and side benefits management that reflected the market. So, for the first salary increase, by conducting very simple planning, I cascaded all salaries within a top-down scale. I found the highest point by taking the highest salary as the median of the highest level and multiplying it by 25 percent. Then, by getting back by 50 percent, I found the lowest point. After that, I passed it on to a subgroup, and I created a pay scale based on titles by founding the median by going down 20 percent of the first-level median. Perhaps this was too simple and did not reflect the market, but to put this system into use, which made the internal order subject to a regulation, we determined the way to adjust the salaries. We did not change the current salaries but rather structured the future. So all concerned managers were okay to go with the system. Two years later, the managers' conversations made it clear to me that the system had been well established. Directors were talking about the salaries on the market within the framework of the rules we had set. Thus, by proposing to make an adjustment upon participating in salary surveys, I made the company switch to a completely correct salary management. If I had implemented the correct salary management at the beginning, the system likely would not have been accepted, and managers would try to bypass the system. It would have been much tougher to get back to the correct system.

The above example shows how HR should plan to achieve their ultimate goal gradually, but there are also negative instances regarding the same situation. For instance, if there is a step to take to change the culture or values of the company, the system will reject the change if it is not ready for it. Even if it is really positive, change becomes impracticable if you do not follow up with concerned departments in a timely manner. When change is put into practice, there should not be any question marks in employees' minds, and HR should test these via pilot schemes. For these kinds of changes, the key is to "walk to talk." Top management, and then middle management, should be the ambassadors of the change. The system does not buy in and change behaviors simply because HR launches them or management believes in it. A child who does not study much, does not care about dinnertime, and has issues at school is likely the product of family values. Therefore, simply saying "Study more," "Come to dinner," or "Act civilized in school" is not going to change his behavior. Punishment makes the situation even worse. You as adults must start acting the way you describe so the child will follow what you are doing. Companies are no different. We were all children once. We follow the leader. To change behavior, you need to set rules for all and act as one, punish as one, and reward as one. Managers love setting rules but not applying them to themselves. In companies I worked for, management used encouraging words, how important people are and so forth. However, their private health insurance policy was much better for top-level management employees. The message between the lines was "Our health is more important than your health." Why would the employee believe in what you are saying in that case? The employees were facing unpaid health invoices and health-related family issues. As HR, we proposed to have one level of health insurance for all and asked the insurance company to keep an administrative fund for us so that we could pay uncovered serious health bills.

Changing behavior or value does not start with message. It starts with setting rules for all and practicing them constantly at all levels, for years to reach the desired value and behavior. Then you don't even have to mention it. It automatically embeds itself in daily life.

HR should practice new applications in a periodical order. This order is a process that should be managed patiently. One should not hurry and get the starting sign about what should be done at which time from the system instead of waiting for a result. HR should not say, "I know when to do it." It is not in your hands. You have to follow the rhythm of the acts to make it better every day.

26

Management Doesn't Empathize

EQ (emotional quotient) is indispensable for management. Feeling without intelligence is better than intelligence without feeling.

Emotional intelligence is not only a characteristic of human but also a core value of companies. In companies where the culture possesses lower EQ, management tends to focus on tangible facts and ignores the human side of the organization. This can be seen often if HR's infrastructure is not strong and managers are allowed to apply their own understanding. Healthy management and human factors are left aside. In this case, the company loses its ability to create long-term plans and strategies. In addition, there is no systemic and uniform behavior. It changes from one department to another. This might not appear to be a problem as long as company makes profit in the short term, but it becomes harder to get persistent performance in the long run.

The best way to ensure a sustainable success story in any company is a well-structured HR infrastructure, supported by an effective E2E system. This is the only way the company will balance humans and business management. There are so many systems provided by I/T companies. The company should establish the most convenient one for the culture and also tailor it to its needs, not to what the system provides. Generally, this topic is disregarded by management and even HR. Companies pursue payroll or related systems as the major investment of HR I/T. In companies with 300–400 employees, Excel sheets are mostly used. The system should push for functions like managing processes, giving periodic feedback to the manager, conducting performance interviews, and preparing the succession system.

HR has a crucial role in the good management of these processes, and in the compulsory empathy system's imposition on management. HR should determine the processes and ensure to make sure applications are practiced. A unique system should have the following:

- Payroll management
- Administrative management, document management, etc.
- Organization structure management, including grading
- Compensation and benefits management
- Recruitment system
- Onboard system
- Performance management
- Talent management and succession planning
- Training and development management
- Reporting system
- Self-services for employees and managers
- Budget and planning, including manpower planning

This is a basic list all HR systems should contain, and they should be integrated to have HR employees act proactively, so managers can be easily involved in HR matters. Only then is it possible to establish the desired culture and eliminate or minimize the individual differences of managers in managing employees. Without this we cannot talk about the same culture or values.

This is a long-term program. HR should be patient to set it well. First, the new system should be applied manually and tested. Otherwise, the company ends up reinvesting the system until it reaches the final necessary one. If the manager does not practice, she gives up on doing it. If the manager has a high EQ, she perceives that need and begins using it. For others, it will not be used.

A typical approach for sales organizations is to apply empathy only with customers. It is obvious that a salesperson should empathize with the customer to establish good relations. However, when it comes to the employee, this is ignored. Employees should feel that necessity with the human resources processes and the infrastructure it has established. They have to feel secure, understood, and recognized.

Knowing the customers, spending time with them, creating a friendly relation and so on are all signs of EQ (or at least acting as if one has EQ). Sales focuses on selling; therefore, managers only pay attention to targets and numbers reached. HR relates bonuses and promotions to target achievements only. For a better managerial style, the focus should change. The company should evaluate managers not just in terms of sales but also in other fields. In cases where the criteria for good management is high performance in all fields, such as investment in people, operational risk, and collection of revenues, then we have complete managers rather than sales managers.

To manage a performance system, a company should know what it wants strategically. In some organizations, there is no HR department. For companies focused on sales activity and that have no other purpose, the key to success is performance. That is how the culture has evolved. In hotel management, for example, if you only pursue selling rooms and making sales, you will lose. As the human being is a product, you have to process it; otherwise, the human becomes a machine. You should maintain balanced criteria, such as whether one oppresses others while making sales or whether one improves others.

Organizations are living beings. Humans are the ones who manage them and put them together. When this situation is not institutionalized, all systems may change whenever a new manager comes in. HR should tell management that employees are humans as much as managers and need to be systematically recognized, noticed, and solicited for their opinion to improve themselves.

27

Fit and On Time

If the system does not understand, then let things flow. In this case, HR should keep warning the system.

Unfortunately, management may decide to apply changes on the business side, especially on the sales forces, which leads to failure at the end. Management hires consultants and spends a good amount of money and effort to design such systems. Meetings after meetings are held, task forces established, and depth analysis performed to get it right. In particular, human resources should be at the table from the beginning in the financial sector to shape it correctly. If this is not the intention, the project will likely worsen the situation or even create a bigger project. So the company ends up going in circles. Expectations are not met, employees become unhappy, stakeholders start to complain, etc. Management does not trust their own experts but rather relies on consultants.

To have a positive transition, the company should follow the steps below together with human resources:

1. Diagnosis: The change needed is considered because something is not going right financially. Without a financial problem, companies do not set out to make big changes in the way they manage the company. So they take reactive steps to decide on a new normal. If it is happening for the first time, they do not question the current organization or management; instead, they choose to go for system changes, hoping that things will do better and results will come.

In fact, the most important step is to understand the real issue and try to come up with solutions that persistently solve the issue. The best way to make the right diagnosis is to ask employees. It's that simple! This is because mistakes usually come from management; the decisions a company makes about products, sales techniques, processes, or marketing are not made by the employees. The main responsibility, in reality, lies with management. Employees or even middle management, in most cases, are actors working by set rules. Why would we ask the same management to create a solution for the issues they created? Depending on the company culture and how strong HR is in the organization, HR should take the lead and arrange workshops and listening sessions to let management know what the real issues are. As a facilitator, a consultant would be helpful. There could be some solution recommended that would not be taken as a way to overcome the problem, since those affect the current status of management and require some changes organizationally and managerially. Then the general manager or even the shareholders should take the lead to have the final word on the solutions. My experience is that this part is usually ignored, and real solutions are not even tested. This is deferring your real problem for another spring. But believe me, it comes back harder than the first time around.

2. Task force: Once we have established the problem correctly, it is time to solve the issue with a well-designed plan. To do this, we need to establish a productive taskforce or project team (whatever you want to call it). We need employees who face the issues, employees not only in favor of management but also the ones who question management's style. They are going to be our opponents. Also, talents are important to have. At this point we may also need a consultant, possibly the one we used for the diagnosis stage. I would also recommend a sponsor team, depending on the level of the problem. I would recommend keeping it at a high level, general manager or similar level. Choose experts who have actually worked on the issues before. One of the experts should be from HR. Of course, we also need a project manager who is known to be a good change agent in the company. She does not

need to be from the related department. This team should consist of no more than ten people to keep discussions and teamwork at a productive level.

3. Roadmap to change: I am not going to explain this part in detail, since we all know how to plan change, but some things are usually ignored in change roadmaps. One is the communication plan. I believe a well-set communication plan is much more important than what is going to be changed. If people to not understand the change, the result will not be reached. So do not ignore this line. It is also important to involve a bigger population of employees who will benefit from the change. A task force should plan to create "ambassadors" of the change. Finally, always target short wins along the road. Change should be felt within three to five months after you launch it.

4. Implementation: Implementing the roadmap requires attention to detail. The task force should continue to monitor and work together during this stage. If there are deviations from the main plan, or if pilots do not show the expected results, the task force should create a "B" plan to make it possible. By the way, pilots are usually used to tell management that the change is working. But what is important is not to create an isolated environment with the best employees just to be able to say it works well. I suggest doing three pilots. One in an isolated environment, another one in a worse environment, and final one in the best possible environment to compare results and make the necessary changes.

Companies who choose not to follow this path will select the wrong solutions for the wrong problems. It will take them years to find out the real problem. To protect their current status, management disregards the problems, hoping they will go away by themselves, until they all hit the wall together.

28

HR Should Support, Not Hamper!

HR should pave the way for making the new manager's life easier and give support, not hamper the manager.

If company does not have written rules, it takes too much time for a new manager or an employee to discover the system in order to survive and increase their performance. Employees are looking for a partner to know things that they need to learn. In particular, the talent we hire get lost along the way if do not help them to be part of the team. They are not included in the discussions, not included in important meetings where they can contribute, and put aside by experienced and senior employees and managers. In one of the conferences I attended, I heard about some research that basically said, "Do not hire the stars of another company." This may sound strange at first, but when you think about it, talents are talents in their own culture and environment. They show their performance under the environmental conditions of the other company. And it becomes harder for this new employee to show the same performance within the new environment and new culture when you hire them. Later on, these employees leave the company when they find out that they will not be able to be successful, as they cannot adapt to the new system.

Therefore, human resources should set up support systems for the new employees upon their arrival. These may take different forms. Corporate camaraderie is one of them. For instance, a senior manager may be assigned to the newcomer to guide the new employee as a mentor, and they may keep in touch. It does not have to be the direct supervisor; a different supervisor might even be preferred.

Apart from this, human resources should create a follow-up program to touch base with the new employee to check how they are doing. This will keep them attached to the company. In addition, orientation trainings are important. We can set up meetings between the employee and the managers so that he can meet them and enlarge his network.

If the newcomer does not get approval from the other managers, then he can hardly be successful. It is crucial for the newcomer to know the elements of the company. Who does what and how? Human resources should even give some tips about the meeting style, information about the working atmosphere, and comforting assurance, for example, "Feel free to give HR a call at any time." The problem is less bothersome for mid-level managers, because the system accepts mid-level managers more easily. But nevertheless, orientation training will make the mid-level manager closer to the others too.

When human resources does not develop these tools, the employee is left to their destiny. That freedom sometimes works well within the system, depending on the department, or it will work against the employee, making her look for alternatives as she is not happy. For the company, this means the loss of an employee who could have otherwise worked out. While practicing these techniques, HR should not regulate as if taking the employee under its wings. It should show the ways and methods of the company to the newcomer in a corporate manner. It should set the rules and follow up on whether they are working. In the meantime, it should lead the employee towards the system with some tools that are based on the employee-manager relationship. On the other hand, it is not good to make the employee dependent on human resources. The key is finding balance.

While hiring managers, cultural and structural compatibility is considered more important than the ability to adapt to the company. For this reason, adaptation and orientation are important issues at manager recruitments. One of the good KPIs would be to have a post-hiring turnover rate trend for the first year to see how many hires leave the company. These ratios are important to keep hiring investments at a healthy level.

29

Career Planning vs. Improvement

If the career planning is not parallel to improvement, the employee will experience a fall after a while. The gap between the two will grow.

Lately, career planning has been one of the most important problems facing companies. Especially for companies with few employees, opportunities to move up are scarce, and it becomes harder to get a higher position despite good performance. It is easier to create new career opportunities in companies having growth trend or high populations, since there are many positions.

Career advancement upward movement, not lateral movement. When a sales department manager is transferred to the accounting department at the same level, he is not considered to have advanced in terms of his career. It is only possible to advance by upwards movement. For the employees, "career development activity" is not much different from saying, "There is no position upwards, so let's advance laterally." I am not saying that lateral moves should not be done. However, planning to move to another level should be well managed after the current lateral move. Only this way we can guarantee understanding and willingness to go for lateral moves.

Lateral moves are excellent to educate employees for middle- or senior-level posts, where jobs get more complicated, and know-how in many different areas of expertise becomes a must to ensure good performance. Therefore, it would be good for human resources to put programs in their succession planning where employees and talents are moved cross-functionally and encouraged to move. You can even make it a mandatory rule to say having cross-functional knowledge is necessary for manager-level jobs. If not as a suggested road in promotion systems. The system should absolutely question cross functional move while promoting and give priority to the ones who achieve it. Promoting an employee to such a position so that she gets this experience will provide motivation, as she knows that she is being prepared for senior levels, even though it is not an upward movement. On the other hand, it will have more significance, as more important steps should be taken for promotion to senior levels. An employee will attach more importance to lateral movement when she finds out that promotion will be possible following a lateral movement.

Naturally, employees want promotion for a better salary, benefits, and empowerment, but I believe that what the employees really want is increased recognition in the eyes of management. This means participating in meetings more, having more say at the meetings, etc. Although this is a temporary measure, human resources may control and manage the promotion request of the employee, bearing in mind that there are fewer opportunities for advancement to the senior level, by inviting talents or good performer employees to projects, creating an opportunity to work with management and attaching incentives, like project bonuses, to encourage them and satisfy their expectations.

As previously mentioned, positions now need more detailed know-how. In this case, career planning becomes harder. Career-based improvement activities should come into play. The most important management technique is to combine career path with improvement. This means making the employees' career parallel to their educational improvement by binding promotion systemically to self-improvement and personal success.

The "training with credits" system is the most efficient of these practices. The employee will act bearing in mind the sum of credits he should get in return for the training required by his current position and the credits he will collect by attending each of these trainings. This way, his own career will be in his own hands. Promotion will be possible only if the employee is successful at the training. To increase assertiveness of the training process offering a simulation of the target environment at the end of the training as the final exam will bring better understanding if the person is really ready.

The employee will be much more focused on development and pay the most attention to development. There should be a pre- and post-evaluation on the improvement of knowledge to prove that the employee will pass the training. A simulation should be used as a tool to measure the behavior, testing whether the employee has learned the information and picked up the necessary behavior. It should also see if the employees have made behavioral progress in other fields.

It is also recommended to develop a program that includes homework, a classroom check with a facilitator, and follow-up activities. In a normal push base training curriculum, training is attached to the managers' requests and mostly left to the managers' discretion. As the training with credit system is introduced, it offers the same chance and requirement for all employees. Then development becomes prominent and not the alma mater (how and where the employee comes from). The system makes eligible only those who have completed the necessary curriculum. Another way of looking at it is to consider training not just a compulsory activity but one of the most important activities in career life, establishing the connection between the system and career as the motivating factor.

30

High Potential Employee = Suicide Bomber

A high-potential employee is like a suicide bomber. If you can't make him stop chasing rainbows, he will damage the system and destroy himself.

High-potential employees are the leading topic discussed in human resources talks, conferences, and company management meetings. This is a process that is managed and cared about by many companies. There are many articles about talent. However, this process is at the same time overrated and puts employees on edge by creating too much tension. High-potential employees are obviously important, but success does not come only from good performance and high potential. Sustainable success and company persistence are provided when the company turns these talents into leaders that lead by performance and also by running teams effectively. So it is important to state how many talents we may have in a company, but it is more important also to show how many we have promoted to let them manage our future. Otherwise it is a "nice to have" list and does not mean much. It can even be a problem.

In this respect, the potential employee should be balanced within a system, not disturb the system, and keep it at the deserved level. We distinguish employees according to their potential. We assess them, train them, and recognize them more than other employees. They are the favored employees. We don't really tell directly that they are talent, but we imply it. One other important point to discuss is that the high-potential employees may not have potential in all fields. This is another mistake we make as managers—believing if an employee is marked as talent, they will go to the moon and successfully create anything we ask. Well, that is not the case!

So what is the solution? The first step is to go from end to start. Why do we want to have talent? Because we need talent to have good employees to manage our jobs. Without them we become fragile and may not plan well the future of the organization. Therefore, talents are security for our future performance and sustainability. The target is to create our own future CEOs and the team that works together with that CEO. Talent is not the ultimate program. It is not important to identify talents and look after them. It is more important to have a program that identifies what we do with them.

There are many ways of selecting talents. Human resources may choose to hire from outside instead of growing them in the organization or create a mixed approach with hiring and also growing within the company or only growing from within the company. None of these are wrong. It depends on your culture and the industry the company is in. Although this is true, there are some drawbacks to hiring from outside, as I mentioned before, in chapter 28. Hiring stars does not guarantee that performance will be there, because we are not in hiring the employee to work in the other company's culture and environment. In the beginning, you won't get the same level of performance. They start to reach the same level later, after they adapt to the system and gain acceptance from others. This is, of course, if they survive. So the best practices to have a ratio of in-sourced and hired employees. One important point for human resources and businesses is not to focus too much on the CV and the success of the person. The questions we should raise should give us an understanding of the personality, the culture they prefer, and the environment they were successful within. But we make mistakes in this regard: we hire based on CV and fire based on attitude.

My experience has shown me that the best way of identifying high-potential is to create a voluntary base system. Firstly, each employee should be given the right to be high potential. Being high potential should not depend solely on the associated manager's preapproval. The employee should have the right to apply to the program. For this reason, human resources should establish a transparent and fair system. Well then, how should we manage this in reality?

As said, the system will be voluntary, transparently announced with a bottom-up approach with all eligibility rules. Then the manager may only comment throughout the process to support the application or not. Even if the manager is not supporting the employee, they should still be going through the evaluation. The comments of the manager should be available only to HR, not the employee. HR should take it as a view of the manager. Let's take the sales department as an example.

Firstly, the department profile should be built up. How are the personalities of the employees who are the leading profiles in the team? What are their models of behavior? These should be determined. These profiles will be the basis for our assessment of the employees. I suggest having functional family profiles, such as finance family. In this family, the company should include finance and accounting for sure but also include the units dealing with budgeting and planning of other departments. Then, differences between the profiles should be analyzed. Human resources should come up with an index system where evaluation basis includes a mixture of things: behavioral assessment, other demographic realities, language credentials, performance track, etc. These should be mixed to come up with a score. If the incumbent is achieves a certain score, a group interview should be performed to mark the employee as a talent. I also suggest segmenting employees depending on their abilities and naming them as "situational potential" instead of "high potential." A high-potential employee at an accounting department will no longer be high-potential if you transfer her to the sales department; that employee would probably not succeed in sales. On the other hand, if we transfer a salesperson to the accounting department, she will likewise not be successful. In this case, we have to manage the perception of the employee would have called a potential.

When an employee is called high-potential, the perception is that the employee is distinctive amongst others, which may make the employee feel more superior than she actually is. This may mislead the employee to such a degree that the relationship with the company is damaged. The employee's relationship with colleagues may be damaged as the employee positions herself as superior to them, and she may boss around or treat others as her subordinates. In the end, that employee might want the entire company to revolve around her. These kinds of employees are like grenades with the pin pulled out—they destroy themselves and everything around them. They cause a decline in performance, and they talk about their position proudly and how they are privileged. They talk about the privileged trainings and benefits they get. Other employees get down, and things get more and more complicated. When a high-potential employee is promoted to a higher level job because they have potential, in reality potential should not be marked as high potential anymore, s/he should prove the system that s/he may perform in the new environment for at least certain years and then to be consider a potential for further positions. However, mostly they still think they are the ex-potential that was marked and continue to be treated exceptionally by the system. Often because this is a new post and the needs are different, their performance weakens. All work entails an adaptation period, and it drags on if the employee has too much sunk into the "high-potential employee" concept, and ultimately everyone runs out of patience. This sounds familiar, doesn't it? If we do not manage these employees, they may poison the positive atmosphere and serve as negative examples to the others, quit their jobs easily, and then feel bad, as they think that can easily find a better job, because they have been flattered. These employees can be discriminated against by managers who are not wise enough. They behave as close friends and try to protect them. When this situation is found out by other employees, the environment becomes nonproductive.

The main theme, which will give striking results, is to avoid calling people high-potential and investigate whether the organization is suitable for succession and managing potential management as a subsystem of succession plans. Potential can absolutely lead to employee success. But being high-potential is not enough. The promotion system should only let employees that get through this system and who are called high potential. Instead of making a single list of high-potential employees, one should make a functional pool if needed. Human resources should set up the systems that will ensure the following:

1. By developing projects and making cross-functional potentials work together, it should increase employees' performance and adaptation.
2. Potential can be recognized as potential by all parties and shown as a common successor for a position if they are known. Therefore, managers from other functions should join the high-potential employee in calibration meetings. This way, the employee should

no longer be department staff. She should be known by the whole company.

3. The system should renew the potential lists every year. Lists should be questioned and updated.

4. Potentials' improvement plans and careers should go hand in hand. Sending employees to expensive training is not a human resources activity. This is taking a step towards turning the high-potential employee into a grenade. Human resources should make a focused improvement plan and manage the improvement activities within this framework.

The potential should turn into an employee who enriches environment. The company should not set up a system that turns around the potential and that support her.

Now, let's talk about an issue I have faced often in my past. We identify talent and also mark them in the succession system as potential successor to a position depending on their credentials and also the feeling of management without knowing what they really wanted to do. This usually happens because we need to keep the pipeline a secret, open only to management and human resources. In order to overcome this issue, we have come up with a simple grid. In the previous company I worked for, we called this the "ability/will" grid. It is a simple means of questioning where talent really wants to be in the future. We asked two simple questions:

1. What other functions do you think you will be able to perform at your best?

2. What really motivates you to work for in the future?

It was surprising to see how many talents marked as successors really do not want to be in that field anymore or are unwilling to do the job. Talents surprisingly switch to another field that they prefer to do. Then, as human resources, we reviewed and matched their credentials to see if they have the ability to do (or can learn) the job in the future. This approach changed our pipeline and also created a good base for cross-functional moves.

The below grid is used to map the talents so that we can use this grid as annex to our analysis.

A group: These employees are motivated to do the jobs they mentioned but have no experience or knowledge on the job. We suggested them for a lateral move to educate them on the matter and also test their ability. There should be a development program supporting the move and ensuring success.

B group: These employees could be immediate successors to the field they mention. Only an adaptation program will align them to the new function. A senior buddy manager can be very helpful.

C group: These employees are the ones we usually make mistake with, by considering them possible successors when in reality they do not want to take the position. Management should find out the reason or ask them to take the job temporarily with the promise that they will be moved to the area where they wish to be.

D group: The talent does not have ability and is unwilling to do the job. These employees usually have problems with their current jobs, with their managers or for other reasons. Since they are identified as talents, it is human resources' duty to find the reasons behind it.

This grid cannot be the only tool to identify the successors but can be very helpful to reach a better decision in succession planning, since it alerts management in advance. If the willingness is low to do a job, performance will be risked, since talent will not say no to the assignment. That is a risk we take as company and find out after the fact.

A	willing	B
the incumbent has motivation to do the job but has no or limited ability to the job	the incumbent has motivation to do the job and also has ability to the job	
not able		able
the incumbent has no ability and also none or limited motivation to do the job	the incumbent has the ability to do the job but has no or limited motivation to do the job	
D	not willing	C

When we have the talents and also set the succession plan, human resources and management should watch out for another fact. FAST TRACK MOVES!

Once the employee is in this pool for any given reason, we appoint them earlier than necessary. I try to explain it in the below chart. Let's say we have three level of jobs: specialist, manager, and senior manager. The requirements different from one to another. Technical requirements, meaning operational experience, is needed at the specialist level compared to the other two levels. On the other hand, managerial ability is needed at the higher level in more managerial jobs compared to specialist job. When we assign a talent in the fast track to upper-level jobs, we may face managerial issues since we expect to see immediate performance from the assignment.

A specialist has little managerial work, as he manages a limited number of employees or does not manage anyone at all. A specialist mostly runs the technical and administrative part of work. He feels he is in the comfort zone with the continuity of the technical work after practicing this job for a while.

If the assignment is earlier than the person expected, they may go back to their comfort zone and still try to achieve success with their known technical abilities. We see this as an issue even at high-level jobs. They continue to ask very detailed questions, take decisions after ensuring what they are doing, and eliminate all risks. They may become managers after a number of years after adapting an understanding the management side of the job. Performance may even decrease gradually, until it finally affects the employee negatively.

Managerial duties			
Technical duties			
Title	Specialist	Manager	Senior Manager

This can be clearly observed in some fields. For instance, IT an employee gets a managerial promotion as their technical skills improve, but they underestimate and ignore the administrative tasks since they have not received this discipline. Only after they are promoted does administrative learning begin by necessity. Once the manager feels confident, she begins to understand the need. As she feels comfortable and competent at her work, she starts to allocate responsibilities and make the employee feel their support; this is mainly led by the self-confidence of the manager. The manager starts learning sooner with the vested responsibilities.

On the other hand, staying in the same position for a long time creates too much self-confidence and blinds the manager. She acts with the idea that "I know everything." The manager ignores the other ideas and become someone who defends herself, does not accept criticism, and loses creativity, innovation, and pace. Finally, performance plummets, because innovation results from desire. The most important part is that the manager knows the employees so well that she cannot make any new decision about them and assessments are reduced to "good" or "bad." When all these combine, performance diminishes in time, the manager herself and the management style take on a narcissistic manner, and the manager ends up believing, "I know the best, I do best, I am the only one."

Well then, how should the manager avoid this?

Ask subordinates the following simple question: "What do you think?" and listen effectively. Employees who have worked at managerial-level jobs for many years might guess the answers to the questions and give the answers themselves. Or they may say to the employee that they tried it before and it did not work. This is, in fact, a kind of narcissism, a feeling of "I know." To avoid this situation, it is crucial to ask questions to employees during the meetings and giving them the right to talk. When you test it, it gets you out of the comfort zone and makes you realize the possibility of thinking in another way. Asking questions is important; however, creating environments where these questions will be asked is even more important. By asking them to manage the projects—especially specialists—and make presentations, the manager will encourage an environment of free discussion. Then manager should be able to read these comments well, by making them practicing, the employees remain open. It is important to grasp the difference. The best gift you can give employees is to make them decide. To do so, you should make sure that they are well aware of the project within small groups, let them observe their managers, and appreciate their efforts. Then employees feel they are appreciated, and they make others feel that way too.

In order to do all these, the process should be in harmony with the management philosophy, which is not easy. You have to be humble, manage wisely, and to know how to observe people. By missing any of these, the manager becomes blunt, spending years in a comfort zone before finally retiring. Receiving queries and being open to challenge is the biggest role of a manager. Standing up to this challenge is one of the most important skills.

Before we finish on the talent-manager combination, I believe there should be systems to support and protect the rest of the employees who are not called high potential, in a direct manner that guides the way. How do we maintain performance and motivation among the rest of the employees?

1. The company may define free career paths. In some companies, there is no way to estimate interdepartmental changes. Experience is highlighted. One cannot switch easily from the sales department to marketing or vice versa. These ways should be kept open; hence, employees should know how to use these ways.

2. Employees' requests can be inquired upon. Generally, managers make the proposal by saying "X is a good employee," but they never ask X or Y what they really want. In fact, the system should find out what employees enjoy doing. Because enjoyment is the origin of motivation, improvement is easier once you enjoy doing something. No one is actually unskilled, but some employees contribute less than others.

3. Internal announcement of jobs can be used. Vacancies can be announced within the company, and employees can apply. If they match the requirements, they can be promoted.

4. There are some jobs that do not need to be managed by high potentials. However, it should be done anyway, maybe even a high-level position. HR should appoint people who have the required skills instead of potential for these kind of positions. These may be experienced and have seniority. A system may put forward these kinds of justifications. In particular, expertise jobs may fall into this category.

31

Should HR Follow Gossip or Get Involved in It?

HR follows gossip but does not get involved in it. It investigates the accuracy and takes note. It does not disclose it. Information matters for HR. It says a lot about the informal structure.

One of the most important tasks of HR is to comprehend the informal structure of a system; the formal structure is already clear. The informal structure may sometimes get ahead of the formal structure. The reason for this is that many companies do not have the elements of the formal structure in a written form. This means that they do not have written job definitions, the configuration of relationships is not defined, and the control structure is not clear. Accordingly, employees find it out and everyone makes his own way, trying to chart it out by experiencing and talking to each other.

Employees know that learning and experiencing "the way" includes gossip as well. In some companies, rumor takes over reality and manages the structure. Therefore, in order to be aware of what is going on and will be happening, they may choose to spread rumors. This can be good and bad at the same time. It is good because sometimes people have to get over things and make sense out of them by talking, chatting, and sharing their feelings. On the other hand, it may be harmful because the topics employees or managers mention usually involve important and secret topics. The main reason companies rely on rumors is that it lacks transparency or changes are happening rapidly and it is not acting fast on the changes. For instance, a planned policy change of sales channel might end up to misleading the sales department of a closure or restructuring rumor if the communication is not managed well. HR should foresee this coming and always use clear communication channels to control the rumors. Instead, human resources chooses not to share the full story. That is where the rumor starts, and it is encouraged by the system. It is better to be open and control the communication. Certainly, it is not easy to give bad news or communicate some changes in a positive way, but the other way around limits the real plan and creates rumors. I have seen managers that thought they would receive new appointments by listening to rumors, increasing their expectations, and acting differently. Then, when reality hits, they resign or lose their motivation to work for the company.

Even if HR transparently all the changes that will take place, rumors will always be around, since people always feel insecure during changes. Consequently, I suggest getting involved in these talks and managing them. This is because information will strengthen plans and also influence employees and managers positively by reinforcing reality. HR should be able to read the informal workspace and manage it differently from one department to another. Each department shows a different attitude towards the change. When HR is aware of it, it should customize the way of communication, informal or formal.

Another issue is dealing with ethical and regulatory violation rumors. Employees tend not to disclose what they hear or even see something happen and keep it a secret to avoid possible harm by mentioning it openly. In order to hear these rumors, humans resources should be a reliable body that acts indifferently. Employees should rest assured that HR will not disclose such rumors. HR's task is not to disclose them to the boss or to the concerned manager but to get the information out of the conversation and analyze the root cause of the problem. For instance, when the gossip about a manager is mobbing another employee or the one telling it to HR manager, HR should have the ability to select the real news out of what the rumor or conversation is. Recheck the truthiness of the mentioned incident. People tend to add their own feelings or thoughts to the conversation, which distracts from reality.

All these are also related to HR's intimacy with the management and employees. If HR is introverted and not in contact with other people, it will be hard to manage these processes. This is because no employee will come and share with HR. Employees only talk about these subjects to people who make them feel close to themselves. Getting out of the office and being active will help the HR manage these processes well.

Another point to be noted is that HR's task is not to support gossip about people and issues; it is to keep that gossip and use it as a channel of communication. Any attempts to kill the gossip will not be successful. Even within a small family, there is a gossip mechanism. Therefore, gossip exists, and it should be managed. If we do not manage it, we will have to face bigger problems. If people are gossiping about an issue, this means there is a problem there. If we close our ears to the gossip, the gossip still continues; we just don't hear it.

Gossip exists at all levels of the hierarchy. As said before, we can avoid it by being transparent and talking about the issues clearly. We must also build trust. If there are systemic fears within the system, then the conversations may mean something other than what we intended. If there is a hidden intention of closing the sales organization (say, by changing the sales channel from grocery store to direct sales) and we don't mention it clearly, then employees may tend to gossip about it. It is discussed so often, at all levels, behind closed doors, that when the reality comes along and company closes some stores, employees conclude that the gossip was true. This happens once, and then next time, they will not believe in the formal communications. You will start to hear people say, "I told you that was really what was happening." It is a vicious circle; it is better discussed openly in the beginning.

32

Warning! HR Is Burning Internally

In HR, when you say the job was not done properly and the employee defends the result by saying, "There was no mistake," raise the alarm! HR is burning internally. The action to be taken is not water but foam.

A good human resources manager should know how to see things from a broad perspective. To do this, when speaking with the customer, HR should know how to look from different perspectives. Otherwise, the comfort zone approach may spread out like a virus and get out of control. An elite HR is the last thing a company would like to have. Regarding this, I once saw something in a company that surprised me a lot. Human resources remained aloof from employees by writing, "Do not call HR" beneath the circular note sent to employees. I think this is the nirvana of being elite as a result of a comfort zone. From that point on, the fire cannot be extinguished with water. At this critical moment, we need to use foam.

One of the biggest mistakes HR can make is to say, "I am correct. The customer is wrong." People work for long years in HR departments, and as they establish the system, they are blindly attached to it, and all the other systems seem wrong to them. They are critical to all changes.

When HR staff experiences this kind of blindness, important changes need to be made, such as rotation to alter perception, new projects, and new responsibilities. There may be even a need for a job change to save the employee. It is really heard to feed oneself by staying continuously at the same place. In one company I worked for, I had a colleague at the managerial level. He was critical and blindly attached to his own rights.

We transferred him to a much lower position. At first, he wanted to resign, rejected the change, but after adapting, he overcame this blindness. When he was promoted to another managerial position after a while, he had great motivation, and he started to make great contributions. HR has to use orientation very well, rotate employees appropriately, and move employee from one function to another one properly so that it does not have to foam. If an employee keeps performing the same job for more than five years, she has been at it for too long; managers will have to keep foaming. This situation kills awareness, and people think they are the best. Sometimes we come across employees who have worked for the same company for fifteen years, and even more, doing the same kind of jobs with the same customer.

On the other hand, for some jobs, technical know-how and skill are important. Those are repetitive jobs (payroll, administration) and do not require a high level of innovative changes. Incumbents of these jobs work by themselves with limited supervision, and cases are solved based on similar experiences in the past. In fields like these, human resources should open specialist positions so as not to lose expert employees. While this contradicts the concept of comfort zones, expectations from the position and the employee are limited in terms of contribution, and the job does not directly address the customer. As this type of job requires more experience and expertise, it is more important to offer good rotation rather than succession. This means human resources should use these jobs to have all new hires work for at least one to two years. This way they will learn the operational side of the job and be supervised by experience managers. At the manager level, the period should not be more than five years. A cross-move may be suggested and will increase management quality. This way we can also ensure that well-performing employees are not blocked by long-lasting managers and choose to leave the company. When a manager manages such expertise jobs for too long, they become indispensable; they control the flow of the job and kill the employees who could replace them in the future. This is the only thing they know and their only way to survive in the company. Human resources should put innovation at the forefront so that it would question the service time. To do so, it should move away hierarchy as much as possible and make sure that every staff has a voice. If the HR manager is in favor of the status quo, she will act as the company rules; however, the employees' requests will not be met.

33

HR Should Make People Talk

If employees do not talk about problems, the unspoken agenda destroys the organization in time and requires a surgery. HR should keep the discussion platform alive.

The system should let the company relieve itself. If not, the company "swells" and needs to be hospitalized. If we do not relax the system from time to time, issues accumulate and turn into a bomb, which is uncontrollable and potentially harmful.

Some systems adore employees who do not talk, who agree with management. This is a very outdated system. There is too much environmental change, and people are exposed to too many things, and they want to express these in their jobs as well. It was hard for us to hear about a kidnapping news from Sudan 30, or live coverage of war, or unfair treatment of people on the streets of another country, or companies in the same sector falling apart years ago, but now we are informed about all facts from all over the world, via social media, news, and other sources. This also becomes an issue for companies to manage, among other managerial tasks. Worldwide communication is too strong. People easily reflect the things they get through this communication in their work life. It is easy for them to correlate these with problems already occupying their mind. We may say things like "Let's focus on our job. What is happening to other companies is not our main concern." If we say that believing it is reality, then it is fine. But if this is just management refusing to open a channel to let people ask questions and elaborate on the issues they are facing, then they will not go away.

Also, there could be managerial problems that we treat as if they do not exist. It is very common in companies not to talk about it, hoping the issue fades away. The less management hears about it, the more they think it is gone, and things are okay now. Well, it is not like that unfortunately. Issues are piling up! Finally, when management hits the wall, these issues are harder to solve.

Human resources should persuade management that even if it does not undertake the responsibility—though that's its duty—it should make sure that employees talk, through workshops and meetings. If the culture does not allow employees to talk freely before their manager, then these meetings should be made with the consultants, and employees should clearly express themselves. Management should find optimizing solutions with the output of these meetings. These should be short-win solutions. HR should analyze the studies like employee satisfaction surveys, internal customer satisfaction surveys, etc., via which the employees express themselves and submit their issues to management, together with the actions to be taken. Human resources should talk to the concerned departments about the actions and seek solutions by mutual agreement. However, one very important aspect of talking to people and asking them to comment is the expectation of action by management. If the action is not going to take place, then the issue becomes bigger. So it is vital to control the action roadmap.

In one company, we faced a terrible sales force ranking in a management presentation. An outside research company presented that we had the worst sales force of the sector. (Or at least it was second-worst.) We were shocked! We believe we were the best and our sales employees were doing their best to reach sales targets and their performance was excellent. However, the results showed that we ranked badly on sales communication, after-sale services, etc. the general manager asked the sales director and me to create a plan to overcome this bad representation. The sales director and I took a short trip outside to think about this. We discussed all the matters around the problem. We decided to put together a program, involving all managers and sales talent, to reshape our vision of sales. We would build a strategy around this and create an action plan where all managers, some employees, the sales director, and HR all took a role. It was a communication of who we are—road shows, training, and reshaping of the way we work. It lasted two years. We took some tough decisions for some managers and employees who did not support the program. After two years, the sales force placed first in the same ranking. It worked!

The key to the roadmap was to establish short wins. Employees realized that ideas change things, and the system began to talk around issues before they got too big to handle.

Management cannot exist if it does not recognize the employee. Managers must understand the employee's needs and what they mean. It is very important to yield to this fact and to keep the way open. Employees like to talk, to be listened to, to argue, and to complain. These should be free and welcomed to do so. Respect should be related to not only opposing and obeying but also to the way and manner of putting forward an opposing view. Human resources should be the pioneer of this attitude.

Conclusion

Human resources is the heart of the company. That is what I believe and what I have seen so far. Working together with more than twenty CEOs and general managers, I have learned that the human resources manager (or director or whatever we call the person in charge) should think like a CEO or GM. This style is at the core of doing a good job as a human resources manager. The second (very important) point is to love "human beings." If you don't like dealing with people issues and being close to employees of any level, you become merely a manager of daily matters and processes. Processes and systems are there to make your daily life easier. The real need is someone who can listen patiently and act fairly and transparently. I have never been afraid of losing my job because I knew what I was doing for the benefit of the company, where all stakeholders benefit eventually. Don't be a manager that everybody loves or everybody hates. If people are all happy with you, you probably are not doing good for the company. If everyone hates you, you're probably too focused on the company's benefit. You need to create a balance.

Always look for improvement in your job, take responsibility, and act. In order to do this, human resources should have a good infrastructure. Simple things should not be difficult to operate. HR employees should spend their time on decisions and relations, not filling out forms and doing administrative work. If you are in this situation, change it; otherwise, you can never be proactive. You may never create a good service level, and the effectiveness and efficiency of the department will be at stake. Develop your people. Don't limit the people attending to outside conferences and training. Those are not expenditures if you plan well and focus your development plans in a structural manner. So, in brief:

1. Educate yourself and follow the development around you.
2. Love talking and hearing employees.
3. Develop your people and keep them updated.
4. Always conduct open and fair dialogue.
5. Be with management and be in management.
6. Act with facts and data.
7. Have an end-to-end system in place that allows HR to be proactive.
8. Keep your door open for your people and employees. Visit them in their places to recognize their being.
9. If you ever bend the rules and create a solution for an employee, industrialize it by creating new rules.
10. Work with a strategy attached to company strategy. If does not exist, then create your own strategy.

We may add to this list, but I think this list captures the basics. Thank you for reading. I hope you found it useful!

About the Author

I graduated from Ankara University in 1980 with a BA degree in economics and commerce. I received my MBA from the University of Bridgeport, Connecticut, USA, in 1982. I started my work life as an auditor in Arthur Andersen, Istanbul, where I worked until 1985. I later joined Interbank, Istanbul, as fund director in treasury, where I worked for five years. In 1989, I joined Coca Cola Co as financial controller and later as bottling HR director. Then I worked for Colgate Palmolive Company as an HR and logistics director. Since 2004, I have been working in banking as a human resources SEVP—first with Yapı Kredi Bank for eleven years before being assigned to Unicredit Bank in Milan for the HR COO position, responsible for operations and projects.

Printed in the United States
By Bookmasters